SIMONE BAGLIONI
STEPHEN SINCLAIR

SOCIAL INNOVATION AND SOCIAL POLICY

Theory, policy and practice

POLICY PRESS SHORTS RESEARCH

First published in Great Britain in 2018 by

Policy Press
University of Bristol
1-9 Old Park Hill
Bristol
BS2 8BB
UK
t: +44 (0)117 954 5940
pp-info@bristol.ac.uk
www.policypress.co.uk

North America office:
Policy Press
c/o The University of Chicago Press
1427 East 60th Street
Chicago, IL 60637, USA
t: +1 773 702 7700
f: +1 773 702 9756
sales@press.uchicago.edu
www.press.uchicago.edu

British Library Cataloguing in Publication Data
A catalogue record for this book is available from the British Library.

Library of Congress Cataloging-in-Publication Data
A catalog record for this book has been requested.

ISBN 978-1-4473-2010-4   (hardback)
ISBN 978-1-4473-2014-2   (ePub)
ISBN 978-1-4473-2015-9   (Mobi)
ISBN 978-1-4473-2013-5   (ePDF)

Cover design by Policy Press
Front cover: image kindly supplied by Shutterstock
Printed and bound in Great Britain by CPI Group (UK) Ltd, Croydon, CR0 4YY
Policy Press uses environmentally responsible print partners

Contents

Preface

Innovation and disruption are defining features of contemporary technological societies. Incessant change, diversity and uncertainty are now considered normal. However, this is a relatively recent and distinctive characteristic of the (post)modern world; for most of human history change was resisted (Diamond, 2013). Today, concern about and resistance to potentially threatening and unwelcome changes are evident across many developed and developing societies. These reactions take various forms – from anti-globalisation protests, and the reassurance offered by various religious fundamentalisms and nationalist movements, to unsettling signs of social tension and anomie (Mason, 2011; Orton, 2015). National welfare systems have struggled to adapt to and cope with some of the challenges raised by accelerating social change. In response to this uncertainty and these new demands, there has been increasing interest in the idea of social innovation as a means to address chronic and persistent social problems.

Our aim in this book is to provide a general critical introduction to the theory and practice of social innovation for an international social and public policy readership. We introduce and explain what social innovation is, and outline the principal features of this intriguing idea. Considerable hope has been invested in and claims made for the potential impact of social innovation. This book will provide readers with the background required to assess the significance of this concept, consider its relevance to social and public policy analysis, and estimate its potential to address social problems and meet welfare demands.

Chapters 1 and 2 clarify the meaning of social innovation by guiding readers through the alternative definitions and different forms that it takes, and discussing how it relates to other concepts, such as technological innovation and social enterprise. For social and public policy analysts, the principal interest in social innovation is whether it offers illuminating insights into established debates or effective responses to social challenges. These include such empirical and normative questions as the relative efficacy of welfare services provided by public, private sector and civil society actors; the capacity of voluntary, community and service user groups to address social problems; and the division of responsibilities between collective and individual, and between self- and social provision of care. The growing prominence of and expectations attached to social innovation therefore raise fundamental questions about the respective capacities of and relations between the public, private and civic spheres in social policy. Reflecting this, Chapter 2 discusses the relevance and implications of social innovation for key policy, research and theoretical debates in social and public policy, and sets out the principal considerations which arise in analysing and evaluating social innovation initiatives.

Moving beyond conceptual and theoretical issues, Chapters 3–5 discuss and analyse evidence about the origin, development and practice of social innovation in three substantive policy areas. Chapter 3 examines social innovation in relation to the issue of food security and poverty. This is a relatively recent concern on the policy agenda of some developed nations, but one of increasing prominence, where a range of civil society organisations have pioneered new forms of provision and developed innovative relationships with corporations and public authorities. Chapter 4 discusses social innovation in relation to social care, another burgeoning challenge for the developed world, but one which conventional welfare states have often neglected. Chapter 5 considers the contribution which social innovation has made to employment policy in response to the labour market transformations generated by technological innovation and globalisation. Each of these substantive chapters considers examples of social innovations which illustrate the key and distinctive properties of this concept, and discuss what such cases suggest in response to the questions posed in the two introductory chapters.

The Conclusion summarises what the evidence presented in these three areas, and the wider commentary in the book, indicates about the significance, strengths and limitations of social innovation, and its implications for social and public policy analysis and provision. The Conclusion also highlights outstanding practical and theoretical issues that must be resolved if social innovation is to make a substantial and sustained contribution to address perennial and emerging social welfare challenges in the UK, Europe and the wider international context.

Both the wicked and intransigent and the new problems which confront societies and policy makers across the world need new ideas, insights and responses. Social innovation is an interesting response to these challenges, and an exciting development in the field of social and public policy. However, it is important that the sense of urgency or the excitement of novelty which often surrounds social innovations does not cloud judgement about the actual impact or potential implications of some of these innovations. We hope that this book helps readers to reach an informed understanding of the potential for both good and ill that social innovation entails, and contributes to a reasoned and evidence-based debate about the future of social and public policy in challenging times.

ONE

Introducing social innovation

The promise of social innovation

The increasing prominence and popularity of the idea of social innovation is in part a reflection of and response to troubled and turbulent times. The challenges confronting established national welfare systems are many and varied: prolonged economic uncertainty and ever-intensifying global economic competition; widening inequality and stagnating or falling living standards for many; technological developments which revolutionise entire economic sectors and transform labour markets; resource depletion and conflicts leading to a migration crisis, depriving lower-income countries of talent and creating frictions in higher-income societies; a pervasive sense of anomie; and, perhaps most threatening of all, a seeming loss of faith in established political parties and institutions, and a corresponding emergence of radical political movements, from the left, right, nationalist and religious perspectives.[1] These challenges have become more acute, while long-standing needs are intensifying or mutating, due to a demographic transition to an older population in the developed North, more diverse and fluid households, alongside increasingly insecure employment and hollowed-out social support systems.

These transformations and challenges are well known (Taylor-Gooby, 2004). However, two striking developments in particular illustrate the nature and scale of the issues which developed national welfare systems now face: population ageing (discussed in Chapter 4) and the transformation of employment (Chapter 5). The developed world is undergoing a demographic transition (OECD, 2012: 13). In Europe the median age is forecast to increase from 37.7 years in 2003 to 52.3 years by 2050, and the ratio of retired to working age Europeans will double over the same period (European Commission, 2013a: 12). In Britain the number of people aged over 85 is predicted to quadruple by 2064 (Carr, 2015: 9). Regarding employment, it appears that, unlike previous waves of innovation (discussed later in this chapter), recent technological developments are not yet generating new jobs at a rate sufficient to replace those they make redundant, and there is concern that they may not do so. It has been estimated that new occupations and emerging sectors accounted for 8.2% of jobs created in the 1980s, but this fell to 4.4.% in the 1990s and to a mere 0.5% in the 2000s. At the same time, almost half of current occupations are judged to be at risk of technological redundancy in the near future (Frey and Osborne, 2013). Some economists suggest that more developed economies are now in an era of 'secular stagnation', marked by chronic low demand for labour and limited economic growth (Summers, 2016). Accompanying (and in part associated with) this is a decline in employment security, progression opportunities and occupational welfare provision (Standing, 2014; Chase, 2015). This post-productive scenario poses dilemmas for social welfare systems: how will those without secure or rewarding employment access resources? And how will care be funded and provided if technology makes entire economic sectors and occupations redundant and employers withdraw protection and social support?

Most societies have used a 'mixed economy of welfare' provision to address social problems and deliver welfare services – involving different combinations of public, private, household and family, occupational, and third sector provision (Powell, 2007). The social or 'solidarity economy' has also played an important role in the welfare mix of many countries. This describes a range of cooperatives, voluntary, professional and/or community-based mutual associations and foundations which combine elements of collective self-help, philanthropic activity, and political and social welfare objectives (European Commission, 2013b: 12). However, in recent years a new term has emerged in the vocabulary of social and public policy, one which some hope will provide new and improved responses to both old and emerging social problems: this is the idea of social innovation. According to the European Commission, 'Europe is facing unprecedented problems that have put in jeopardy its currency, economy and social model. Perhaps at no time since the 1940s has social innovation been so urgently needed' (2013a: 10). There has been considerable investment of political and financial capital in social innovation. However, some caution, if not scepticism, is required in approaching this idea. The first step to interrogating it thoroughly is to clarify what it means.

References to social innovation have become increasingly frequent and prominent (Godin, 2012). It is a concept which has 'been edging ever closer from the outer realms to the central focal point of attention' (Howaldt and Schwarz, 2010: 5). Interest in social innovation is growing within and beyond Europe, and it is now part of the mainstream public policy vocabulary (Reinstaller, 2013: 3). For example, the former European Commission president declared that 'The financial and economic crisis makes creativity and innovation in general, and social innovation in particular, even more important' (European Commission, 2009). The Commission's *Europe 2020 flagship initiative innovation union* described social innovation as its 'overarching policy objective' (2010: 2). Reflecting this, it created a European Programme for Social Change and Innovation (2014–20) and made social innovation central to both the European Structural Fund and the European Regional Development Fund. Similarly, President Obama established an Office for Social Innovation and Civic Participation in 2009, and committed $50 million to social innovation in the 2010 Federal budget.

Social innovation is therefore an idea with many advocates and champions. The Quebec Declaration claims that 'Social innovation enables the implementation of more effective, just and sustainable solutions to increasingly complex social problems' (RQIS, 2011: 4). It is no surprise to find enthusiasm for the idea that wicked and emerging social problems might be solved by harnessing the dynamism of social innovators. Equally, the appeal of applying lessons from business and technological innovation to devise imaginative solutions to intractable social problems is understandable. However, more sceptical commentators suggest that 'it is questionable whether the hype around social innovation and social entrepreneurship can be reconciled, thus far, with a corresponding volume of tangible outputs' (Chalmers, 2012: 20). It is not yet clear whether the level of attention that social innovation attracts is matched by its accomplishments or impact. Our aim in this book is to answer this question. There is growing interest in social innovation from across a range of fields and disciplines (see Moulaert, 2009: 11; BEPA, 2010: 32; Caulier-Grice et al, 2012: 4; Reinstaller, 2013: 5). However, 'SI questions and calls for a review of the way in which the welfare state is to be organised and delivered' (Bonifacio, 2014: 148). Consequently, this book focuses on the implications of social innovation for social and public policy: that is,. the analysis of collective responses to social problems (Sinclair, 2016). We do not cover every aspect of what might be included in the 'social economy' discourse, but we examine how social innovation relates to this more familiar concept, and to the general idea of a 'mixed economy of welfare'.

Social innovation has been described as 'an inspiring concept' but, as it has developed principally through practice, experiment and experience, it has not, until recently, been adequately conceptualised or theorised (Nicholls, 2006; Voorberg et al, 2014). Addressing the continuing gap between action and analysis is another aim of this book, and the contribution which social theory can make to understanding social innovation and improving practice is discussed in Chapter 2. Some of the theoretical and empirical questions which social innovation raises for the study of social and public policy include whether it really marks a significant transformation in either the philosophy or the practice of policy as claimed, and how significant a response it is to contemporary social problems. How does social innovation relate to more familiar concepts, theories and debates in social and public policy? Does it add anything to our understanding of policy processes and outcomes? Do social innovations have any greater or otherwise distinctive impact beyond those achieved by conventional forms of welfare provision? Do they produce any unintended consequences? Social innovation therefore relates to the core concerns of social and public policy: the nature of wellbeing and what constitutes welfare (and for whom)? Social innovation also raises questions about citizenship rights and welfare entitlements, equality, equity and distributive justice. For example, are welfare services delivered more effectively by state, private or civil society actors? It is also an international phenomenon where much of the practice and policy has originated in the developing South. This may create opportunities for sharing experience but also poses questions about the viability of policy transfer and the capacity of institutions to learn and adapt. Therefore, social innovation touches upon such matters as path dependency and theories of the development and dynamics of welfare regimes and families, which are discussed in Chapter 2 (Esping-Andersen, 1991; Castles, 1993; Pierson, 2000).

Finally (for the moment) the phenomenon of 'reverse' or 'trickle-up innovation' – where under-served communities create products and services to meet needs overlooked by mainstream suppliers – raises interesting questions about the responsiveness and accountability of welfare services (Govindarajan and Trimble, 2012). Encouraging and cultivating social innovation could be part of a radical devolution of power and democratisation of social policy making, recognising experiential knowledge and the authority of lay expertise. However, it could also lead to unfair variations in service quality, or to governments offloading the responsibility for social problems onto over-burdened communities. Evidently, therefore, critical engagement with the theory and practice of social innovation is required. Fortunately, there is a growing body of research data and policy analysis which can provide the robust evidence required to evaluate whether the current enthusiasm for social innovation should be welcomed or warned against.

Entrepreneurship and innovation

There is a wide-ranging and extensive literature on social innovation and related concepts, the full range of which cannot be covered here. Nevertheless, to understand social innovation and what it means for social and public policy, it is necessary to consider the development of the concept and how it relates to neighbouring ideas and discourses. This requires brief consideration of innovation in business and technology, and how these relate to the particular notion of *social* innovation.

Creative destruction and waves of innovation

In the field of business, innovation simply means 'doing something new and better' (Sisson, 2011: 9). More specifically, 'Innovation is the application of knowledge to the production of goods and services. It means improved product and service quality and enhanced process effectiveness' (Department for Business, Innovation and Skills, 2014: 5). Analysis of the sources, nature and effects of innovation dates back to Richard Cantillon, Adam Smith and Max Weber, but most discussions take as their starting point Joseph Schumpeter's analysis of the role of entrepreneurs in the capitalist economy, initially proposed in his *Theory of economic development* (2004; originally published 1911) (Howaldt and Schwarz, 2010: 9). Schumpeter argued that the 'incessant innovation' which distinguished capitalism was due to entrepreneurialism, which was the engine of economic development. Entrepreneurs revolutionised production, as they were willing to develop or exploit inventions or use resources in new ways to 'destroy old patterns of thought and action' (Schumpeter, 2004: 85). He elaborated on this in *Capitalism, socialism and democracy*, arguing that:

> the function of entrepreneurs is to reform or revolutionize the pattern of production by exploiting an invention or, more generally, an untried technological possibility for producing a new commodity or producing an old one in a new way, by

opening up a new source of supply of materials or a new outlet
for products, by reorganizing an industry and so on. (1976: 132)

The dynamism of this restless innovation generated what Schumpeter
called the 'perennial gale of creative destruction' (1976: 84), which
stimulated productivity and economic expansion by dispensing with
outmoded processes and products (Okpara and Halkias, 2011: 7).
According to Acton, this incessant change transformed societies and
ushered in the era of Modernity – marked by 'a new order of things,
under a law of innovation, sapping the ancient reign of continuity'
(quoted in Giddens, 1971: xi).

As the quote above from *Capitalism, socialism and* democracy implies,
not all innovations are technological. This is evident from more recent
experience: 'In the 1970s, when American companies were overrun
by Japanese and European competition, it was not so much scientific
– IT was in its infancy – but managerial innovation that led to foreign
domination' (Madrick, 2014). It has been estimated that less than
20% of investment in innovation by UK firms funds what would be
regarded as conventional research and development; the bulk is spent
on innovation in design, branding, training and skills development or
on marketing (Northern Ireland Executive, 2014: 8).

Schumpeter believed that the innovations pioneered by entrepreneurs
and the economic growth these enabled had made a greater
contribution to reducing poverty than either state welfare provision
or charity (Nasar, 2010: 191). The economic and social benefits of
enterprise and innovation continue to be lauded by economists and
governments:

Innovation is the engine of economic growth and improved
living standards ... Innovation has been transforming the world
economy since the industrial revolution ... On the back of
these improvements the time it took to double living standards
dropped from five centuries in 1300, to one century in 1800 and
then to 28 years in 1929. (Department for Business, Innovation
and Skills, 2014: 6)

Schumpeter's theory that business entrepreneurs are the sources of innovation relates to the idea that societies have been transformed by successive waves of innovation in general purpose technologies (1976: 67–8). Although a variety of dates and names for these episodes is used in the literature, five long waves of innovation are commonly identified (Howaldt and Schwarz, 2010: 3; Nicholls and Murdock, 2012: 1):

- the Industrial Revolution – from the 1780s;
  steampower, railways and heavy engineering – from the 1830s
- electricity, chemicals, cars and Fordist production processes – from the 1870s
- electronics, petrochemicals and nuclear power – from the 1950s
- computing, IT and telecommunications – from the 1970s.

It has been suggested that another new wave of innovation is currently underway, based on nanotechnology, a new generation of communications and information technologies and the requirements of sustainable development (Arthur, 2009). It is argued that this new wave of disruption will be driven by 'combinatorial innovation', which generates non-linear, discontinuous transformation through the interaction of various technologies. In particular, it is predicted that an exponential increase in computing capacity (for example, through quantum computing), more powerful algorithms mining larger databases and interacting with machine-to-machine communication (or the 'internet of things') will transform economies and societies (Rigby and Hayden, 2013; Naughton, 2015). These combinatorial technological developments will accelerate the occupational and economic upheavals referred to at the beginning of this chapter and discussed in Chapter 5. Whether they will have a net positive or negative effect remains to be seen, and depends (as in so many other things) on how they are applied, political and policy responses to change, and the resources and opportunities available to different groups.

This reinforces the double-edged nature of innovation. In contemporary society social innovation may sound attractive as 'innovation is often considered as a value in itself' (De Vries et al, 2014: 19). Nowadays, even many so-called conservatives support the novelty and supposed improvement assumed to be characteristics of social innovation (Membretti, 2007). Innovation is equated with progress; to oppose it seems at least sentimental and at worst reactionary and a Luddite opposition to progress. Enthusiasm for innovation and the belief that it leads to progress is a product of the Enlightenment and core to the ideology of capitalism. However, innovation (even the social variety) is not necessarily benign. 'For most of its history the concept innovation, a word of Greek origin, carried a pejorative connotation' (Godin, 2012: 5). Change involves disruption and risk; it may threaten entrenched traditions or cherished beliefs and challenge established power bases. There may be good reasons to be cautious about the stories told about and by innovators and entrepreneurs.

Schumpeter portrayed innovators and entrepreneurs as exceptional beings:

> To act with confidence beyond the range of familiar beacons and to overcome ... resistance requires aptitudes that are present in only a small fraction of the population and that define the entrepreneurial type as well as the entrepreneurial function. (1976: 132)

Some accounts of the behaviour and character of social innovators reinforce this heroic image (see, for example, Bornstein, 2004; William-Powlett, 2014). This tendency is particularly prominent among those who interpret the idea of social innovation as a form of social business, such as those associated with the Ashoka movement established in 1980 by Bill Drayton (Caulier-Grice et al, 2012: 6; see also Drayton, 2004; Yunus, 2008).

However, this portrayal of business or social innovators and entrepreneurs as dynamic visionaries should be tempered by other considerations. One cautionary fact is that many innovations are the outcome not of individual but of collective initiative and are often created by co-production (Sarasvathy and Venkatraman, 2011).

Often the source of invention and innovation 'begins when a worker, customer or client identifies a problem in a product or service and seeks a remedy' (Adams and Hess, 2010: 140). A second objection to the heroic image of entrepreneurs is that it tends to aggrandise private enterprise and denigrate the extent and significance of public sector inventiveness and innovation. Mazzucato (2013) has shown that private capital is often less adventurous than government-funded research. For example, many of the components contributing to combinatorial innovation were initially developed within the public sector or underwritten by government support, with private investors only becoming involved once riskier start-up issues had been resolved. This applies to the internet, the world wide web, touchscreen technology, MP3 systems, nanotechnology, graphene, informatics, and several recent developments in clean technology and biotechnology. In fact, some of these developments only became transformative technologies because they were made public and freely available rather than restricted by private proprietorial rights. Schumpeter himself anticipated both these features, and bemoaned the end of the era of the individual innovative entrepreneur, which he predicted would be superseded by the 'inevitable bureaucratisation of enterprise' (Chang, 2014: 144).

Defining social innovation

It has been observed that 'Social innovation is a term that almost everybody likes but nobody is quite sure what it means' (Pol and Ville, 2009: 881). The varied uses of the term must be acknowledged (Caulier-Grice et al, 2012: 4). In fact, some commentators have become exasperated with this ambiguity and complain that the 'language around social innovation easily slides into smoke and mirrors' (Roberts, 2008), or that 'the concept has been stretched in so many directions that it is at breaking point' (Grimm et al, 2013: 436).

There are considerable difficulties in settling on a definition of social innovation. It not only refers to a very diverse and dynamic range of phenomena (Montgomery, 2013: 1), but it also excites considerable passion from advocates and different schools of thought (Chalmers,

2012: 19). Some commentators and partisans suggest that vagueness is helpful as it means that 'a broad range of organisations and sectors have felt comfortable adopting the term and engaging in the debate surrounding it' (Caulier-Grice et al, 2012: 4). Ambiguity also has the advantage of rendering social innovation empirically irrefutable (Ayob et al, 2016). In this respect, social innovation has a similar conceptual status to the 'social exclusion' discourse in the European Community in the 1980s and '90s (Room, 1995). However, for the idea of social exclusion to become theoretically and empirically valuable, rather than merely politically convenient, it had to be refined beyond being an indeterminate 'quasi-concept', and this is also required in the case of social innovation (Jenson and Harrison, 2013: 10).

Examples of social innovations

Although it is a concept which came to prominence only in the 1990s, social innovation has a much longer heritage; in fact 'the notion of social innovation has existed in various incarnations for almost two centuries' (Benneworth et al, 2014: 3). A wide range of activities and many diverse examples of projects, initiatives and reforms have been described as 'social innovation' (Howaldt and Schwarz, 2010: 7). Examples include the following:

- kindergartens;
- hospices;
- fair trade;
- urban farming[2] – using vacant spaces in built-up areas (often in deprived communities) to cultivate small crops, with produce often distributed to local residents;
- guerrilla gardening[3] – taking over and planting flowers in what are regarded as neglected or abandoned sites for aesthetic and political purposes;
- local exchange and trading schemes (LETS);[4]
- Freecycle[5] – an exchange and recycling network designed to retain useful goods in circulation and minimise waste;

- Women Like Us[6] – a social business supporting employment among mothers;
- restorative justice;
- the Slow Food movement;
- Open University (and distance learning more generally);
- Pratham schools in India – low-cost preschools which employ young women with basic training to provide introductory education for children in low-income communities (Leadbeater and Wong, 2010: 17);
- Complaints Choirs[7] – a semi-comic musical collective, created in 2005 to voice and exorcise minor gripes, which has since become a global phenomenon after becoming an internet meme;
- Alcoholics Anonymous;
- League of Nations;
- European Union.

In the area of financial inclusion alone there are numerous examples and forms of social innovation:

- credit unions;
- the cooperative movement – dating back to the Rochdale Pioneers in 1844;[8]
- the Grameen Bank and microfinance more generally;
- complementary and regional currencies and loyalty schemes;
- time banks;[9]
- participatory budgeting;
- Community Economic Development Funds in the US and Canada;[10]
- the UK government's (short-lived) Child Trust Fund.[11]

Case study: Men in Sheds

Men in Sheds is a project aimed at reducing social isolation and improving mental health among older men. It started in Australia in 2006 but has since expanded internationally, and in 2015 there were an estimated 700 such projects in the UK alone. The project brings older men together to apply and develop their practical skills in repairs, DIY, woodwork and related tasks. The products made and services offered are sold to generate the resources required for facilities and equipment, and local projects aim to be self-financing and independent of subsidy.

Approximately one million people in the UK say that they feel always or sometimes lonely, and about five million people have described their television as their main source of company (Spear and Moss, 2015: 17). In relation to health and wellbeing, loneliness and isolation are more hazardous than obesity, and the impact on life expectancy is the equivalent of smoking 15 cigarettes a day. Men in Sheds provides opportunities for social interaction and stimulating rewarding work which enhances self-esteem for a group which is particularly vulnerable to loneliness.

It is clear that the term social innovation has been applied to a wide field, varying scales of activity and diverse organisational forms. Some of these examples may seem far beyond core areas of social and public policy, but they are all related in some way to wellbeing in a wider sense. Social innovation has therefore been described as a 'portmanteau concept' (Benneworth et al, 2014: 7), and the concern voiced that 'false definitions, ideals and descriptions are superimposed onto a phenomenon or initiative with markedly different origins and motivations' (Edmiston, 2015: 7). More positively, it has also been interpreted as a 'supercategory' which 'integrates what would otherwise be separate activities and inquiries' thereby enabling issues and actions to be reframed (Harris, 2005: xi). However, to achieve this more positive effect, it is necessary to consider what the different examples described as social innovation have in common, and clarify what unifies and distinguishes this concept from others.

Standard definitions of social innovation

Although social innovation has been a contested and controversial concept (BEPA, 2010: 33), there has recently been an emerging consensus about its principal elements (Ayob et al, 2016). A definition associated with the Social Innovation Exchange (SIX), the Young Foundation and NESTA in the UK has increasingly become accepted as a standard version. This describes social innovations as 'innovations that are social both in their ends and in their means' (European Commission, 2013b: 5; see also SIX and Young Foundation, 2010: 18). A more elaborate version of this is:

> Social innovations are new solutions (products, services, models, markets, processes etc.) that simultaneously meet a social need (more effectively than existing solutions) and lead to new or improved capabilities and relationships and better use of assets and resources. In other words, social innovations are both good for society and enhance society's capacity to act. (Murray et al, 2010: 3; and Caulier-Grace et al, 2012: 18)

This definition is important because it has come to underpin the European Commission's approach to social innovation. It is also the best-known and clearest example of how two alternative interpretations of social innovation have recently converged: one which focused on social innovation as *process* or means and emphasised the social relations that social innovation reproduces (particularly cooperation and co-production), and another which prioritised *outcomes* and the social impact of social innovations (Moulaert, 2009: 12; Grimm et al, 2013: 436; Bonifacio, 2014).

Despite this emerging consensus, there are some obvious problems with this definition of social innovation. First, it is tautological and unsatisfactory to use the very terms which are to be defined by a concept in the definition of that concept (Franz et al, 2012: 4). Second, this definition begs another question – it cannot be known in advance that a social innovation will 'meet social needs more effectively than alternatives'. Impact can only be known after the innovation has operated effectively for at least as long as these alternatives (and once any unintended side effects are known) (Evers et al, 2014: 11). Some of these issues are drawn out in Chapters 3–5; however, for the time being the defining features and core elements of social innovation merit more detailed consideration. Combining various accounts, these can be condensed into three components:

1. Content or product: what the social innovation does to address unmet social or environmental needs
2. Process: how the innovation does this – the mechanisms, actions and governance applied to effect change
3. Empowerment: the nature of user involvement – how social innovations mobilise groups and cultivate positive social relations to enhance capabilities and increase access to resources (Gerometta et al, 2005; Moulaert et al, 2005: 1976; Caulier-Grice et al, 2012: 13)

Principal characteristics of social innovation

Social orientation

As the name makes clear, what distinguishes a social innovation from other forms of innovation is that it 'has as its starting point notions of social beneficence' (Dawson and Daniel, 2010: 11). Social innovations are not incentivised by the profit motive or exploiting market opportunities per se, but reflect moral and political values and address social or environmental concerns, such as quality of life, wellbeing, social exclusion and distributive justice (Okpara and Halkias, 2011: 1; Bonifacio, 2014: 147). Social innovations are also established to meet genuine needs, not to generate or stimulate new desires among potential customers, as is the case with conventional capitalist organisations ('demand engineering'). This feature has potentially radical implications and marks social innovation as an alternative to the capitalist ethos – where the pursuit of profit and competitive imperatives mean that enterprises often devote considerable ingenuity and resources to inventing and serving potentially damaging demands (Akerlof and Shiller, 2015).

By this measure, neither corporate social responsibility (CSR) nor ideas of 'shared value' (Porter and Kramer, 2011) would qualify as social innovation, although some commentators have described both as such (Phills et al, 2008). Neither of these activities (nor such innovative market activities as emissions or pollution trading) alter the fundamentals of corporate practice; rather, they remain conditional upon a business case or have purely philanthropic and charitable foundations. In contrast, social innovation is driven by a social mission, in addition to its other defining characteristics.

Social innovation as a response to 'failure'

Social innovation is often described as response to unmet need – either chronic neglect and delivery failures, or a response to some new challenge (NESTA, 2007; Harris and Albury, 2009). For example, the former president of the European Commission suggested that social innovation involves tapping creativity 'to find new ways of meeting pressing social needs, which are not adequately met by the market or the public sector and are directed towards vulnerable groups in society' (Barroso, 2011: 2). Social innovations are therefore attributed to market and/or public service failure (Seelos and Mair, 2005: 48), so that their very existence is an implied criticism of existing practice (Nicholls and Murdock, 2012). Chapter 2 considers some aspects of the implied critique of public services. However, it should be noted that some of the service gaps and 'opportunities' made available to social innovations have been generated by corporate and/or government decisions. One example which illustrates this is the labour market deregulation policies pursued in several countries over the past 30–40 years. Until the early 1980s, many large employers in the UK and the US assumed (or were obliged to assume) that they had a responsibility to protect their staff's living standards in various ways, including paying adequate wages, maintaining relatively secure employment and providing various forms of occupational welfare. In contrast, in the US today about one in three workers are not directly employed by the companies principally identified with the product on which they labour, but work instead for subcontractors or are hired through various agencies and classified as self-employed (Weil, 2014). The result of redrawing responsibilities in this way is the precarious employment described earlier in this chapter, and the employability and labour market social innovations developed to respond to this, which are discussed in Chapter 5.

Borzaga and Bodini (2012: 8) caution against describing social innovations as addressing market failure, as this might suggest that what distinguishes them from private enterprises and economic innovations is an indifference to profitability. In fact, some social innovations do seek and make profits (for example, fair trade, microfinance); however, they do so not exclusively but in conjunction with other imperatives (Caulier-Grice et al, 2012: 9). Nevertheless, this raises a more general point about the limitations of markets to serve needs which are unsupported by effective demand. Taking this point further, some social innovation theorists argue that it should be related to a broader sustainable development approach to economic thinking which incorporates wellbeing considerations and transcends the division between 'social' and 'economic' objectives (BEPA, 2010: 37).

Innovation as novelty

The word innovation seems to imply novelty and suggest that social innovations are unprecedented. However, social innovations need not be entirely new. Some may use long-established models and methods, as in the case of credit unions (traceable back to at least the 1850s). Other social innovations may apply established technologies or processes in new ways or to new issues. Social innovations may also involve creating a distinctive combination of existing features, known as 'recombinant innovation', that is, 'taking something from somewhere else, and using it in a different way' (Hartley, 2014: 229), or what William-Powlett describes as 'stealing with style' (2014: 11). There are many examples of this in the social innovation literature, such as the *Le temps pour toi T* ('Time for Roof') and *ESDES Inter-Générations* projects in France, where cheap accommodation is provided to young students in intergenerational homes, where they interact with and provide support to older residents (see Chapter 4) (Evers et al, 2014: 18). There is nothing original about generations living together and looking after one another. But in the context of contemporary dynamic households and potentially fragmented urban areas, it takes a social innovation to bring together diverse and potentially estranged groups to (re)create mutual care relationships and rebuild community bonds. This is also an example of a social innovation which addresses multiple issues: the housing needs of a low-income group (in this case students), the risk of isolation and care needs of older people, and renewing social capital. This illustrates the fact that 'often the most exciting social innovations occur at the edges or interfaces between sectors' (Bonifacio, 2014: 148).

Invention and innovation

Several accounts of social innovations emphasise the importance of their practical effects:

> social innovation is defined more by impact than by 'newness' ... We see this as a crucial feature. This is because social innovations are not just new solutions, they are new solutions that work better than existing practices and therefore bring about measureable improvements for the populations they serve. (Caulier-Grice et al, 2012: 9–10)

Social innovations are more than merely promising ideas, they are 'the process by which new ideas turn into practical value in the world' (Dawson and Daniel, 2010: 14; Casebourne, 2013: 20). A distinction is often drawn between invention, which involves the creation of an original procedure or technology, and innovation, which is the adoption and effective application of an invention. Apple Inc. became one of the most successful companies in the world on the basis of innovation rather than invention: it did not create the technologies upon which the success of the Macintosh computer nor the iPod and iPhone were based, but redesigned and marketed the inventiveness of others.

Inventions become innovations (social or otherwise) either through unplanned diffusion or deliberate and active dissemination (Greenhalgh et al, 2004: 15). This highlights the importance of both informal networks and formal incubators, hubs and knowledge brokers in the generation and spread of social innovations (discussed in Chapter 2). The impact of innovations is also dependent upon their viability and sustainability: a social innovation cannot simply be a one-off idea, no matter how original or good it may be; it must also have the potential to be replicated and scaled-up to 'have durability and a broad impact' (Moore and Westley, 2011: 1; Borzaga and Bodini, 2012: 8). This has led some theorists to argue that social innovation must ultimately be institutionalised and routinised to sustain its transformational impact (Howaldt and Schwarz, 2010: 26). From this perspective, the ultimate aspiration of the social innovation is to become absorbed within a mainstream which it has transformed. At this level, social innovation overlaps with social movements and processes of social change more generally. Both this relationship and the challenge of institutionalising innovation are discussed in Chapter 2.

Innovation v incrementalism

Innovation means more than minor modifications or merely rebranding existing practice (BEPA, 2010: 40; Hartley, 2014: 227). 'Innovation is properly defined as an original, disruptive, and fundamental transformation of an organization's core tasks' (Lynn 1997: 154). Innovation entails a discontinuous change or 'a radical break from the past' (De Vries et al, 2014: 5). Innovation does not mean simply doing the same thing better, but doing things differently or doing different things. Innovations are therefore disruptive and transform the 'basic routines, resource and authority flows and beliefs of any social system' (Westley and Antadze, 2010: 2). Such a fundamental challenge to established perceptions, practices and systems will inevitably provoke opposition, an issue discussed in Chapter 2. Resistance to innovation is not necessarily reactionary or self-serving. As mentioned above, there may be legitimate grounds to resist the upheaval which innovation entails, including the value of protecting the continuity of essential services. There are also potentially considerable costs and risks involved in disruptive change and 'Some very interesting innovations are not successful' (Hartley, 2014: 227). For example, it is estimated that about one in three innovations in the private sector fail to deliver anticipated improvements (Tidd et al, 2001).

It is also worth noting the exacting standards required of social innovation from this condition: stimulating transformational systemic change is a relatively rare accomplishment. There are many seemingly successful and sustainable initiatives that could be regarded as social innovations which may not have fundamentally transformed a situation but are no less valuable. For example, it could not be claimed that *The Big Issue*, or other street newspapers providing opportunities for homeless people, have transformed the property market, the social housing system or prevented homelessness. However, they have certainly been an innovative way to support many vulnerable people and perhaps may also have changed the attitudes of some readers towards homelessness. It may therefore be necessary to temper both expectations of and some of the more grandiose claims made for social innovation.

Participation and empowerment

Many advocates of social innovation emphasise their participatory and empowering qualities. This is what is meant by describing social innovation as being innovative in 'both its goals and its means' (BEPA, 2010: 9). For example, the former European Union commissioner László Andor, stated that 'social innovation is not only about finding alternative solutions to gaps in the market and public sector, but it is about finding the best ways to empower people – especially deprived groups – through their active involvement in the innovative process' (2011). Social innovations address unmet needs by inclusive means, developing and reinforcing communities or creating new collaborative relationships which enhance social capital (Mulgan et al, 2007b: 35). Social innovations bring people together, 'creating new and sustainable capabilities, assets or opportunities for change' (Adams and Hess, 2010: 144). This investment in and cultivation of individual and collective capabilities can also produce relational goods: non-material benefits and assets which can only be produced and consumed or enjoyed collectively (Franz et al, 2010: 13–14). The paradigmatic example of a relational good is a choir, but many other organisations, associations and social innovations share this quality (such as the food banks discussed in Chapter 3).

As a social innovation is defined as much by an empowering process as by its social purpose or impact, it must involve participants in more than a tokenistic way; in fact, some would argue that genuine social innovations must be user-led initiatives. The former EU Commission president proposed that a 'successful innovation ... is something you do with people, not to them' (quoted in BEPA, 2010: 57). This relates social innovation to the literature on service user involvement and co-production, discussed below (see, for example, Beresford and Carr, 2012). An example which illustrates this aspect of social innovation is the 'Neighbourhood Mothers' project in Berlin discussed in Chapter 4. This is a network of women trained to provide advice and support to migrant communities by liaising between this marginalised group and public authorities and service providers (Evers et al, 2014: 17).

Ayob et al (2016) identify two social innovation traditions which contrast on this issue of participation and empowerment. The first 'radical' tradition places strong emphasis on the social relations enabled and enhanced by social innovation. This is exemplified by Moulaert et al, who identify a 'social rationale' of social innovation in promoting social inclusion alongside an equally important 'political rationale' of giving voice to marginalised groups (Moulaert et al, 2005: 1970). In contrast to this there is a utilitarian social innovation tradition, associated with theorists with a business school background and interest in private enterprise, which focuses much more on the social mission and value proposition of social innovation (see, for example, Phills et al, 2008). Although the radical perspective attaches much more significance to social innovation as an overt collective movement, participation and empowerment are essential and not incidental features of all definitions of and approaches to social innovation. The Capability approach defines capabilities as those outcomes which individuals have *reason* to value, meaning that informed choice and agency are integral features of genuine capabilities (Sen, 1985). A capability-enhancing social innovation must therefore enable participants to shape services to reflect their freely chosen needs, otherwise service users are mere passive recipients of initiatives controlled by others. Despite this, it has been noted that their contribution to empowerment 'is one of the most under researched and under-explained aspects of social innovation' (Caulier-Grice et al, 2012: 20).

Classifying social innovations

The lack of a settled definition of social innovation suggests that it is at a pre-paradigmatic stage of development. Therefore any discussion can only outline the contours of a landscape – its general topography and prominent features – with rough and disputed borders. Social innovations are examples of 'hybrid organisations', which possess the characteristics of more than one sector (Billis, 2010). Such hybrids have increased as policy makers and social innovators create new multi-sectoral responses to address complex issues and challenges.

There have been several attempts to classify and codify social innovations using various criteria and dimensions (see, for example, Hämäläinen and Heiskala, 2007; European Commission, 2013b: 7). We draw upon several such accounts (BEPA, 2010; Nichols and Murdoch, 2012; De Vries et al, 2014) to organise social innovations according to three criteria:

- form of innovation, for example, a new idea, concept or way of thinking; a new product, process or technology; or a new organisational form;
- degree of innovation, for example, distinguishing what Bateson (1972) described as a 'second order change' involving examining and changing assumptions (such as a new business model), from a 'third order' paradigm shift which transforms how the nature of an issue is conceived and dealt with at a societal level;
- scale of innovation, for example, from addressing local issues or operating at a small scale geographic level, to regional, sector-wide reforms (such as banking or housing systems) up to international social movements.

As it is an ideal-typical classification, the divisions between these dimensions cannot be exact and actual social innovations could be assigned more than one description. Nevertheless, these dimensions cover the wide range of social innovation examples listed above and included in the literature, while reflecting their scale, scope and varying degree of originality, and also preserving the defining features of a social innovation: that is, their social purpose, element of novelty or distinctiveness, sustainable impact and empowering participants.

Figure 1.1: Classifying social innovations

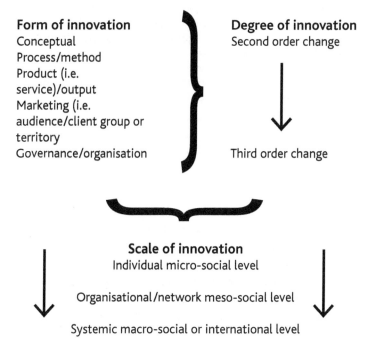

Form of innovation
Conceptual
Process/method
Product (i.e.
service)/output
Marketing (i.e.
audience/client group or
territory
Governance/organisation

Degree of innovation
Second order change

Third order change

Scale of innovation
Individual micro-social level

Organisational/network meso-social level

Systemic macro-social or international level

Case study: the circular economy

The idea of a circular economy and principles of circular design illustrate some of the characteristics of social innovation. The circular economy model contrasts with a linear approach to production, which assumes that resources are abundant and disposable. In contrast, a circular economy approach designs products and processes to minimise resource use and waste. It applies the principles of recover, recycle and regenerate, and adopts a whole-life approach to the production, distribution and exchange of goods and services. This might involve transforming a business model from selling finished products to leasing services to customers. Such a change replaces the incentive for producers to create inbuilt obsolescence with an incentive to design products for maximum longevity and minimal maintenance, thereby reducing resource depletion.

'Social innovations are inherently about changing the way things are done and the way social needs are conceptualised' (Norman et al, 2013: 9). The circular economy is a social innovation in this respect, as it involves a paradigm shift in process and production design. It is motivated (in part) by environmental and social concerns and combines these with a commercially viable business model. It is also replicable and scalable and could potentially have a systemic transformative impact. However, it need not necessarily empower service users per se. Therefore although it is innovative and possesses several of the defining components of a social innovation, it is perhaps best regarded as a mode of production compatible with social innovation, rather than a social innovation itself.

Social innovation and social enterprise

Distinctions between social and other forms of innovation or such concepts as the solidarity economy cannot be rigid or absolute. There are 'blurred frontiers' in particular between social enterprise and social innovation (Defourny and Nyssens, 2010: 42). This is complicated by the fact that (rather like social innovation itself) social enterprise is a 'fluid and contested concept constructed by different actors promoting different discourses connected to different organisational forms' (Teasdale, 2011: 1). The terms 'social entrepreneur' and 'social entrepreneurship' were first used in the 1960s and '70s (Steinman, 2010: 20). The idea of a social enterprise as a trading association with a social purpose was developed by Spreckley, who described it as follows:

An enterprise that is owned by those who work in it and/or reside in a given locality, is governed by registered social as well as commercial aims and objectives and run co-operatively may be termed social enterprise. Traditionally, 'capital hires labour' with the overriding emphasis on making a 'profit' over and above any benefit either to the business itself or the workforce. Contrasted to this is the social enterprise where 'labour hires capital' with the emphasis on personal, environmental and social benefit. (Spreckley, 1981: 8)

Somewhat different ideas of social enterprises and social businesses – with less emphasis on cooperative ownership – were subsequently developed by Bill Drayton, the founder of Ashoka (Ridley-Duff and Bull, 2011). There remain different strands and schools of social enterprise with different emphasis on social and economic activities and cooperation (Teasdale, 2011). This difference in emphasis corresponds roughly to European and American approaches to social enterprise, although there are many exceptions to this pattern as well as other international variations reflecting distinctive cultures and traditions.

The Scottish Social Enterprise Network (Senscot) uses five criteria to distinguish a social enterprise:

1. Social mission: social enterprises are motivated by social and/or environmental objectives.
2. Enterprise: social enterprises are trading businesses aspiring to financial independence. A social enterprise should generate 50% or more of its income from trading rather than depend upon public sector grants or subsidies.
3. Asset lock: social enterprises re-invest all distributable profits to pursue their social objectives. No more than 35% of their profits should be distributed in dividends to shareholders.
4. Independence: social enterprises cannot be the subsidiary of and must be constitutionally separate from any public body; however, they can be a trading subsidiary of a charity.
5. Values: social enterprises behave ethically towards their stakeholders and ensure staff have appropriate wages, terms and conditions.[12]

These criteria are broadly similar to the definition of social enterprise used by the EMES research network, which is particularly influential in European debates (Borzaga and Defourny, 2001).[13] It also resembles the principles of social business proposed by Muhammad Yunus, the founder of the Grameen bank and credited with developing microfinance.[14]

It is clear from these definitions and criteria that social innovation covers a much broader range of activity than social enterprise (Caulier-Grice et al, 2012: 7; Montgomery, 2013: 1). Prominent examples of social innovations which are not social enterprises (that is, they have no business activity) include Alcoholics Anonymous and the Red Cross. Some social entrepreneurs may form enterprises which deliver socially innovative programmes (Caulier-Grice et al, 2012: 7). Alternatively, social enterprises may disseminate or develop the commercial aspects of social innovation (Ayob et al, 2016: 13). However, social enterprises need not be particularly inventive or innovative (some follow models developed decades if not centuries ago) and social innovations need not be particularly enterprising in a business or commercial sense.

Public sector innovation and intrepreneurialism

Most discussions of innovation focus on the private or third sectors, but as was noted above, there is considerable innovation incubated within and by the public sector and social innovation may also be nurtured there (Moore and Hartley, 2008: 3; Caulier-Grice, 2012: 11). Much of this involves sharing ideas, resources and practices across sectors (Adam and Hess, 2010: 147). Examples include public sector bodies creating spin-off organisations to deliver services, or forming joint ventures with private or community sector partners. For example, 58% of local authorities in the UK own a trading company and 57% operate a joint venture with the private sector (Carr, 2015: 7). It is estimated that such activities made up 6% of local authorities' budgets in 2012/13, amounting to approximately £10 billion. This sum is anticipated to rise to 18% of councils' budgets by 2020 – totalling roughly £27 billion (2015: 7).

Such activity might be interpreted as the straightforward privatisation of public services, but in some cases these inter-sectoral shifts are accompanied by more obvious social innovations. A defining feature of social innovations is that they are 'developed "with" and "by" users and not delivered "to" and "for" them' (Caulier-Grice et al, 2012: 22). This principle resembles aspects of co-production of services, community budgeting and 'localism' in policy making and delivery (Stoker, 2005). Community and participatory budgeting feature prominently in many accounts of the history of social innovation. Participatory budgeting was pioneered in 1989 in Porto Alegre, Brazil, when the Workers' Party devolved decision-making to communities to improve the accountability and responsiveness of local public services (Moulaert et al, 2005: 1984; Harkins and Egan, 2012: 5). The principles of transparency and citizen control which participatory budgeting –and related ideas of community planning – promotes reflect the view that there should be a two-way relationship between citizens and service providers. Champions of social innovation in public services argue that in post-Fordist social and economic systems old divisions between production and consumption no longer apply (Bason, 2010). Instead, service users increasingly demand to be treated as 'prosumers' – involved in design and delivery, and no longer merely passive recipients of what others decide to provide (Toffler, 1984). This tendency is most evident in the phenomenon of open innovation (Chesbrough, 2003). In an open innovation system, 'Citizens and customers no longer serve as suppliers for information about their needs (as in traditional innovation management); they make contributions to the process of developing new products to resolve problems' (Howaldt and Schwarz, 2010: 17).

One example of public policy and service co-production in the UK is the Beacon and Old Hill estates in Cornwall, where residents became involved in designing and delivering community services (Scottish Government, 2010: 9). These are areas of high and concentrated deprivation which have been subject to a succession of conventional (and largely unsuccessful) regeneration and social inclusion initiatives. With the support of local health officials, the residents of the Beacon and Old Hill estate were invited to identify their priority concerns and lead the development of responses to these. What emerged from this dialogue was an organic and improvised policy-making process, as one commentator described:

> The most significant aspect of the regeneration process on the Beacon and Old Hill estate was that, from the outset, there was no initial funding, no hierarchy, no targets, no business plan, only a shared vision of what the community wanted to be, rather than an obsession with what it had to do. Thus, the regeneration process was not a result of a predetermined plan. Rather, the process emerged as a consequence of the interactions between the members of the community, and between the community and its environment, namely the statutory agencies, the police, the council, and so forth. As the community evolved, so also the agencies and professional bodies co-evolved with the community. (Durie et al, 2004: 285)

This is an example not only of service co-production leading to social innovation, but also of public sector intrepreneurialism, that is, policy reform initiated from within institutions. Such consultative and cooperative decision making are central principles of design thinking, which is an increasingly important source of social innovation. Design thinking involves addressing service failures which result from not consulting nor collaborating with users:

> Time and again, initiatives falter because they are not based on the client's or customer's needs and have never been prototyped to solicit feedback. Even when people do go into the field, they may enter with preconceived notions of what the needs and solutions are. This flawed approach remains the norm in both the business and social sectors. (Brown and Wyatt, 2010)

User engagement and co-production are core principles of design thinking. This recognises the grounded and experiential expertise of communities and service users as the starting point from which to understand issues and develop responses. Consequently, effective design thinking involves democratising the authority to shape how issues are conceptualised and solutions framed.

However, intrepreneurialism, design thinking and participatory policy making are particularly challenging for public sector organisations, where statutory duties, performance regulations and concerns about political accountability often inhibit risk-taking. In these circumstances policy and social innovation may be eschewed in favour of tokenistic and symbolic participation. This issue is discussed further in Chapter 2.

Case study: social impact bonds

Some of the defining features and issues raised by social innovation can be illustrated by considering whether social impact bonds (SIBs) should be regarded as an example of social innovation.

SIBs lever private finance (usually brokered by a third sector intermediary) to fund public services. If the service meets its targets (usually by performing better than conventionally funded services) then investors get their money back and also receive a dividend payment. This bonus is funded from the estimated future public expenditure savings made by the improved performance (for example, the lower costs of reduced crime achieved through an SIB-funded probation and rehabilitation service). If the service fails to achieve its targets then investors lose their money. The logic behind SIBs is that funders will ensure that service providers focus on meeting performance targets and that the potential taxpayer costs of innovation are reduced. SIBs are therefore portrayed as a 'win-win' for investors, service providers and taxpayers (McHugh et al, 2013)

SIBs are certainly imaginative, and they might generate additional sources of investment and create new institutional relationships. However, whether they constitute a departure from existing policy or an incremental development on existing 'payment-by-results' policy models is a matter of interpretation. The question of whether SIBs empower service users is even more contentious. This is not an issue considered by many of their supporters, as SIBs take a 'black box' approach to service delivery. This means that policy makers set the targets to be delivered but do not specify how results should be achieved. Because what matters is the outcome rather than the process, SIBs do not necessarily empower service users, but in fact treat them as a means to an end – not as citizens but as commodities (Sinclair et al, 2014).

The SIBs example shows that policy innovation is not necessarily the same as social innovation.

Conclusions

This chapter introduced and tried to explain what social innovation means and how it relates to more familiar concepts and ideas. Chapter 2 discusses how social innovation relates to particular debates in social and public policy. Social innovation is certainly sufficiently prominent in the contemporary social and public policy discourse to require the attention of analysts and scholars. However, we asked at the beginning whether it is a significant new development in theory, policy or practice, and whether its impact justifies the attention it has received. Evidence relevant to answer these questions is provided in Chapters 3–5, and reflected upon in Chapter 6. To put the significance of social innovation into perspective it is helpful to have some way to measure the extent of policy change. Daigneault (2014: 416) provides a useful framework to assess the scale of policy movement. According to this framework, a genuine paradigm shift in policy involves substantive change across four dimensions:

- values, principles and assumptions about the nature of reality, for example, ideas of justice, the proper role of the state and so on;
- conceptualisation of the problem;
- ideas about which policy objectives and outcomes to pursue'
- ideas about the most appropriate means to achieve outcomes.

Some of the theories and models underpinning particular social innovations possess some of these qualities, but currently social innovation is too diffuse a phenomenon to qualify as a paradigm shift. Social innovation currently exists discursively as much as it does in reality – it is a term used to (barely) encompass and locate a diverse range of activities and initiatives rather than to describe a clearly demarcated set of interventions and institutions. While there are many examples across the world of flourishing and effective social innovations, it is questionable whether they are sufficiently similar to be subsumed within a coherent concept. Social innovations may be an example of a 'magic concept', that is, an idea with 'A high degree of abstraction, a strongly positive normative charge, a seeming ability to dissolve previous dilemmas and binary oppositions and a mobility across domains' (Pollitt and Hupe, 2011: 641).

Their supporters claim that 'Social innovation often recognises, exploits and coordinates assets and resources which would otherwise be wasted, under-used or not used at all' (Caulier-Grice et al, 2012: 23). Resource efficiency is a virtue often claimed for entrepreneurs and innovators: they supposedly direct investment and reallocate assets to emerging activities and sectors where they may be deployed most effectively. However, in the case of social innovation, this is a question to be examined empirically rather than purported as fact. It is also a proposition premised on a fairly simplistic economic conceptualisation of productivity, one which does not apply to complex social problems and welfare services, where there is often no single bottom line or simple efficiency calculus. It is therefore not a straightforward task to establish whether social innovations offer better responses to social problems and welfare needs than more established and conventional responses. Nevertheless, the examples and evidence considered in Chapters 3–5 illustrate some of these activities, and Chapter 2 outlines some of the social and public policy questions these raise.

As the former European Commission president pointed out, 'Social innovation is not a panacea' (quoted in BEPA, 2010: 14). However, he also went on to claim that 'if encouraged and valued it can bring immediate solutions to the pressing social issues with which citizens are confronted' **(2010: 14)**. This remains to be seen. Imaginative responses are certainly required to address the social and economic challenges outlined at the beginning of this chapter, but whether social innovation is itself the solution, or can inspire better responses, requires considered analysis and some caution.

Case study: El Sistema

El Sistema, a musical education programme developed in Venezuela, illustrates several of the key features of and issues raised by social innovation. El Sistema describes itself and its mission as 'an intensive youth music program that seeks to affect social change through the ambitious pursuit of musical excellence' (El Sistema, n.d.). Since being founded in 1975 by José Antonio Abreu, El Sistema has become internationally lauded and led to the creation of the acclaimed Simón Bolívar Symphony Orchestra. It also claims to have provided musical training to over 700,000 children and young people. The aims and method of the programme are undoubtedly innovative (although not necessarily entrepreneurial in a business sense). Providing free musical training and orchestral experience to very deprived children is also clearly collaborative and potentially empowering; and the initiative has been the vision of a charismatic and energetic founder. The appeal of El Sistema transcends conventional political divisions, as opposing perspectives can focus on different features which they find attractive. The movement's leaders and spokespeople have skilfully exploited this wide-ranging appeal by emphasising different characteristics to different stakeholders. For example, during the period of Hugo Chavez's government, El Sistema's leaders highlighted the collectivist ethos of orchestral musical education, and downplayed references to the pursuit of excellence per se, in order to pre-empt potential accusations of cultural elitism.

Understandably, the accomplishments and recognised musical excellence of El Sistema have attracted enthusiastic support (Tunstall, 2013). However, some of this praise is based on questionable evidence. Indeed, it would be difficult to ascertain what 'success' for El Sistema entails, as it is difficult to define, let alone assess, its multiple, mixed and fluid aims.

The impact of El Sistema was made possible by extensive government support and private subsidy (Kenyon, 2015: 74). The intensive after-school musical training which is central to the programme is also made possible because the Venezuelan education system allows children considerable free time in the afternoons and evenings. These features raise questions about the autonomy, independence and transferability of El Sistema, questions which it shares with many other social innovations.

The musical education which El Sistema provides to young people undoubtedly enhances their skills, but it does not necessarily mean that they are thereby empowered. Although El Sistema has had a profound impact on the personal and social situation of the most accomplished performers, this is only a small proportion of the children and young people it has reached. For the majority, there has been no transformation in their circumstances or conditions in their communities. It is perhaps unrealistic to expect a musical education programme to have such an effect, but this gap between the acclaim and impact which El Sistema has achieved is something it also shares with other similarly high-profile social innovations.

Finally, El Sistema faces the challenge of sustainability and maintaining what success it has achieved over the longer term. The problem of surviving beyond the contribution of a charismatic social innovator and how to negotiate the transition from being a maverick outsider to a mainstream member of the establishment are issues which confront the most successful and high-profile social innovations.

Notes

[1] 'Many authors have developed different aspects of the historical transformations which the world economy is going through. Hamalainen and Heiskala sum it up to five factors: the "information society", the globalisation or [sic] economic activities, the increasing specialisation, complexity and knowledge intensity of production processes, the growing differentiation of demand patterns and the development of cooperative arrangements".' (BEPA, 2010: 32)

[2] www.urbanfarming.org

[3] www.guerrillagardening.org

[4] www.letslinkuk.net

[5] www.freecycle.org

[6] www.womenlikeus.org.uk

[7] www.complaintschoir.org

[8] www.rochdalepioneersmuseum.coop

[9] www.timebanking.org

[10] See www.cedf.com

[11] www.gov.uk/child-trust-funds/overview

[12] www.senscot.net/view_art.php?viewid=9636

[13] http://emes.net/

[14] www.grameencreativelab.com/

TWO

Social innovation and social policy

Introduction

The previous chapter noted the widely held view that 'Social protection schemes and policies in the Member States are at a turning point' (European Commission, 2013a: 17). Loss of faith in both the state and private sectors, and dissatisfaction with Fordist welfare systems and services, underlie growing interest in social innovation (Edelman, 2015). Some believe that more flexible local services are better suited to meet the needs of contemporary complex, diverse and dynamic societies (Grimm et al, 2013: 448–9). However, although these challenges, and those considered in Chapter 1, explain the current prominence of social innovation they do not themselves prove that it offers the most effective response. There are other options available and considerations to be taken before promoting social innovation as an alternative to conventional public service provision. This chapter outlines the questions which social and public policy analysis pose for social innovation (Sinclair, 2016). First, there are normative questions about whether social innovations might really be the best way to enhance welfare. Second, analytical and theoretical questions concern the origin and nature of social innovations – how they come about and function. Finally, as applied disciplines, the most important questions of all in social and public policy analysis are evaluative: are social innovations more cost-effective than conventional welfare services? Are they better able to address the needs of disadvantaged groups? Chapters 3–5 discuss what the research evidence in selected areas and cases tells us about some of the answers to these questions.

Theorising and thinking about social innovation

Social innovation 'is a practice-led field' (Caulier-Grice et al, 2012: 4) where much of the accumulated wisdom has been generated and is possessed by frontline practitioners (Cumming, 2008). Consequently, there is some scepticism about what contribution theories can make to social innovation, with some critics suggesting that 'any general theory is likely to be either banal or wrong' (BEPA, 2010: 32).

Despite such scepticism, theory is necessary to inform and improve the practice of social innovation. Theories generate hypotheses about relationships between factors which can be empirically examined. Such relational and causal hypotheses inform reflections upon experience and emerging evidence, allowing outcomes to be sustained or improved upon. Furthermore, all social innovations are based on an (often implicit) understanding of how the social issues and problems which they address come about and how society functions. For example, microcredit initiatives, such as the Grameen Bank, are based on (among other things) the idea that entrepreneurial self-help (such as starting a microbusiness or investing in education) will reduce poverty. Consequently, Muhammad Yunus and other social innovators have devised imaginative new ways to improve access to credit and financial services for excluded and impoverished groups. While the achievements of the microcredit movement are considerable, there is still widespread and entrenched poverty in most of the countries in which they operate (Bateman, 2010). This raises the question of whether microcredit is based on a plausible diagnosis of the principal causes of poverty and offers an effective remedy to whatever these might be. The important issue to consider in examining any social innovation is what is its underlying theory of change and what does it suppose are the principal causes of the problem it addresses? Without such a theory, the trial-and-error approach characteristic of many social innovations may become a wasteful hit-and-miss enterprise.

Therefore, while practitioners and enterprising social innovators may have pioneered the development of social innovation, analysts and theorists contribute by posing questions, developing hypotheses and gathering data to advance understanding of how social innovations function and what impact they have. Experience suggests that such theoretical contributions are more likely to be valuable if they focus on some of the specific questions social innovation raises rather than try to construct grand and abstract theories (Sinclair and Baglioni, 2014).

Until recently, a lack of robust evidence inhibited the development of theories about the operation and impact of social innovations. As several commentators have observed, much of the discussion of social innovation has been 'based on anecdotal evidence rather than on scientifically proven fact' (BEPA, 2010: 42). The majority of studies have been qualitative case studies with relatively few comparative analyses (De Vries et al, 2014: 20). Sceptics have criticised the tendency in the social innovation literature towards 'romanticizing achievements and potential; simplifying or ignoring limitations, trade-offs, dilemmas and contradictions; and downplaying the political and institutional drivers of progressive change' (Utting, 2013). Many social innovations do not have clear aims and objectives, and do not set themselves measureable goals, making it difficult to assess their success. Attributing outcomes to particular social innovations is difficult enough, let alone comparing these to the impact of alternative initiatives and more conventional programmes (Brandsen et al, 2016: 4). However, an increasing number of rigorous and systematic comparative research studies are moving the social innovation debate beyond anecdotal to scientifically robust evidence.[1] In addition, the development of such techniques as social return on investment (SROI), social accounting and social audit processes are helping to address the evaluation gap (European Commission, 2013a: 18). Nevertheless, while these approaches enable the impact of individual social innovations to be estimated, they do not provide a picture of the collective and cumulative effects of the social innovation sector at the macro-social level; nor do they show whether it produces greater social benefits than existing or alternative options.

Case study: Social Return on Investment

Social Return on Investment (SROI) is a form of cost–benefit analysis which assesses the added economic and social value directly or indirectly attributable to a social policy or initiative. Although not necessarily concerned with attaching a monetary value to social outcomes, this has become the principle use of SROI (Costa, 2017). The technique is increasingly popular in evaluating the costs and effects of social innovations, as it considers outcomes which go beyond conventional economic impact assessments.

SROI is based on several principles and procedures:

- involving stakeholders in determining what is selected for measurement and how measurements are made (for example, relevant evidence on inputs and outcome);
- outlining a theory of change and impact map which delineates how resources and activities relate to outputs and outcomes;
- using this impact map to identify what to evaluate – stakeholders should be consulted in ranking the relative importance of different outcomes in terms of their respective economic, social and environmental benefits and costs;
- developing proxy measures so that monetary values can be attached to each selected outcome;
- considering how to attribute outcomes to activities, estimating deadweight (that is, what would have happened without the initiative), and taking account of potential displacement effects and any drop-off in impact over time;
- not over-claiming by comparing any identified outcomes with alternative policy options;
- transparency: explicitly outlining the assumptions made and evidence used to attribute and measure outcomes;
- verification: ensuring that outcome estimates are independently scrutinised and cross-checked.

The strengths of SROI are also its weakness: it reduces the evaluation of complex interventions with diverse outcomes to a common (usually monetised) set of measurements. While this enables assessment of the relative cost and social effectiveness of initiatives, it does so potentially at the expense of simplification.

Social innovations may be imaginative, but innovation is not necessarily the same as improvement. Social innovations must therefore be assessed using the general criteria which apply to all social policies:

- Normative: Does the intervention correspond with important moral principles, for example, is it just and equitable? Does it promote solidarity and/or community cohesion? Does it avoid moral hazards and unfair rewards?
- Outcomes: Does the intervention meet stated objective and targets?
- Empowerment: Is it emancipatory? Does it enhance service users' capability?
- Value for money: Is it more cost-effective than alternative options?

Normative social innovation questions

Any social intervention raises normative questions, and social innovation is no exception. The most fundamental social policy question is what constitutes wellbeing and, by implication, what contribution does any particular social innovation make to improving human welfare? (Bonifacio, 2014: 148). Social innovations cannot evade fundamental questions of social justice, the principles of fair distribution and the basis of social rights. Analysing social innovation therefore involves considering what are (and ought to be) the respective competencies of the state, market and third sectors in reconciling what Keynes described as 'the political problem of mankind: how to combine three things: economic efficiency, social justice and individual liberty' (1926). Although these moral questions are fundamental to social and public policy, they cannot be explored at length here (Spicker, 1988). Nevertheless, they reaffirm that social and public policies involve far more than mere technical considerations – they are guided by moral deliberations and judgements of what constitutes human wellbeing and a healthy society (Galbraith, 1997; Sandel, 2009).

In addition to expressing and reaffirming social values and principles (such as desert, entitlement, reciprocity, contribution, solidarity etc) there are more practical considerations involved in evaluating social innovations and other social interventions. Any assessment of whether a social innovation is a more effective and efficient response to social needs than conventional welfare services must bear in mind that these services perform multiple functions:

- providing access to essential services, for example, sanitation, housing, etc;
- meeting basic living needs, for example, preventing destitution and alleviating poverty among those unable to secure an income through unemployment, sickness, disability, old age, etc;
- providing help to meet additional expenses,for example, those associated with bringing up a family, disability, etc;
- caring for the vulnerable, for example, children, the infirm and incapacitated;
- enabling independent living and enhancing capability, for example, through education and healthcare provision;
- operating as a 'lifetime savings bank' by redistributing income from periods of employment and earning to spells of economic inactivity (Hills, 2014);
- supporting social cohesion and integration, for example, through community regeneration;
- contributing to economic stability and growth, for example, by enhancing the health, education and training of a skilled and productive workforce; enabling labour market flexibility and risk-taking, etc.

As this extensive list of functions demonstrates, welfare services and policies have both micro- and macro-level effects. Therefore a further question asked of any social innovation from a social and public policy perspective is how well it meets these multilevel purposes and demands.

One reason for some of the enthusiasm shown for social innovation is the criticism that conventional forms of welfare provision only compensate for losses or meet needs after they arise, rather than prevent problems occurring. Proponents of social investment approaches to welfare criticise conventional services as 'passive' and allege that they are at best partially remedial responses to problems (Morel et al, 2012). It is argued that rather than intervene after damage has already been done, welfare services and social protection systems should, as the former UK Secretary of State for Work and Pensions put it, transform lives and promote resilience (Duncan Smith, 2012). There is therefore growing interest in developing more proactive approaches to welfare and moving 'upstream' to enhance immunity against social problems and prevent them arising (McKinlay, 1975; Sinfield, 2004). Some hope that social innovation might enable such a proactive and preventative welfare system by replacing familiar and allegedly unsuccessful deficit models used by asset-based initiatives (Mendelson, 2007). This aspiration is reflected in the emphasis placed upon service user empowerment and co-production in the social innovation discourse. It should be borne in mind that criticisms of conventional welfare provision as passive and reactive might be ideologically motivated (Friedli, 2011). Nevertheless, their capacity to promote resilience and enable preventative interventions should be added to the questions asked of social innovations.

Analytic social innovation questions

Do social innovations emerge from certain common conditions or develop in response to unique specific local issues or circumstances? Are they the product of particular entrepreneurial individuals, or created by networks or other social relationships? It is of more than academic interest to answer these questions and understand where social innovations come from and why they develop where and when they do. Understanding how social innovations come about and which conditions facilitate innovation is essential to developing a social innovation support strategy which could cultivate them systematically, should this be considered desirable (Sisson, 2011: 3).

In the private sector, innovation may be spurred by a threat or crisis. Changes in circumstances – for example, the emergence of a new competitor or market opportunity, new consumer demand or some other extraneous risk – may challenge existing business models. Such exogenous challenges oblige private enterprises to revise their business models in order to exploit opportunities, to remain competitive or even to survive. Comparable external shocks are the inspiration for some social innovations. One common spur to third sector innovation 'is significant loss of income, forcing organisations to ask themselves whether they can deliver the same or better outcomes for less money by rethinking their approaches' (William-Powlett, 2014: 11).

However, innovation can also be a proactive and positive change rather than merely a response to threats. Investing in research and new product development is an obvious example. Beyond the business sector, only the largest third sector organisations possess the resources required to research and develop new products or services through formal research. However, this need not be a handicap to innovation, as many ideas for new products and services in the private sector originate not from research but from feedback from customers and frontline service providers (Von Hippel, 1988). In this respect, any organisation open to input from stakeholders should, in principle, be able to innovate. Indeed, given their emphasis on co-production and service user empowerment, this source of innovation ought to be stronger among social innovators. It should also be given added impetus by the growing organisational interest in and public expectation of open innovation (discussed in Chapter 1) where users 'are deeply involved in generating new products' (Franz et al, 2012: 13-14).

One challenge to intentionally cultivating social innovation in particular is that it is often organic and spontaneous, arising from particular experiences and specific local challenges (Moulaert et al, 2005: 1972). Furthermore, innovation is rarely linear (Caulier-Grice et al, 2012: 37). Many social innovations emerge and evolve through trial and error in response to experience rather than follow predetermined strategic plans. This improvised development makes inferring general and transferable lessons difficult, and is another reason why practice has preceded theory in social innovation. It is difficult to be certain which conditions will best enable social innovations to germinate and grow. Although this is one knowledge gap that comparative studies are beginning to address, there are still unanswered questions about which legal or regulatory environments are most conducive to enable a flourishing social innovation sector (BEPA, 2010: 11).

Case study: MindLab

MindLab is a government-funded innovation incubation unit in Denmark which brings together citizens, private businesses and other stakeholders to develop new solutions to social challenges. MindLab describes itself as 'a physical space – a neutral zone for inspiring creativity, innovation and collaboration'. Design Thinking principles are central to how it operates: 'MindLab is instrumental in helping key decision makers and employees view their efforts from the outside-in, to see them from a citizen's perspective and to use this approach as a platform for co-creating better ideas which generate value for citizens' (Northern Ireland Executive, 2014: 14).

Its director, Christian Bason, has described his vision of how social innovation can be enabled by and within the public sector:

- moving from a random to a conscious and systematic approach to innovation;
- changing policy makers' role from administrating public organisations and managing human resources to building innovation capacity within and beyond the public sector;
- shifting from running tasks and projects to orchestrating co-creation processes which develop new solutions in partnership with rather than for people (European Commission, 2013a: 14).

Similar social innovation incubators and partnerships have been established in several other countries, for example, the Centre for Social Innovation in Toronto, the Melting Pot in Edinburgh, the Philippi Village business park in Cape Town and the Basque Centre for Social Innovation in Bilbao, which is partly supported by the Mondragon cooperative.

These examples testify to the importance of participation in networks and public support in the cultivation of invention and diffusion of social innovations.

One increasingly evident finding from studies of innovations is that they are rarely created by single individuals but emerge from complex interactions and immersion within networks (Sisson, 2011: 3). The work of Castells (1996) and others shows that creativity and innovation are processes embedded in particular environments or innovation milieux, where new developments are generated by creative synergies and disseminated through supportive cultures (Florida, 2002). The creation and development of innovation through networks reflects Schumpeter's (1976) conclusion that innovation was no longer created by individual visionaries (discussed in Chapter 1). The increasingly collective nature of entrepreneurship and innovation is reflected in the fact that relatively few recent technological innovations are associated with or named after a single inventor (Chang, 2014: 246). Innovation requires relational resources which extend beyond individual enterprises and involve exchanges between customers, frontline staff, researchers, professional contacts, investors, banks, universities and think tanks, and the third and public sectors (Howaldt and Schwarz, 2010: 11; Gretzinger et al, 2015: 81). Going beyond this, some commentators argue that innovation is stimulated by the creative tensions produced by inter-sectoral exchanges: 'Research shows that new knowledge and different ideas are more likely to emerge when diverse actors that do not normally interact closely with one another come in contact with each other' (Moore and Westley, 2011: 4).

Social innovation and welfare regimes

Innovation might not only be generated at the boundaries between sectors but may shift these boundaries themselves. Social innovations can take the form of or result in new inter-sectoral partnerships, hybrids and spin-offs, thereby complicating how 'public' and 'welfare' services are conceptualised. This has implications for theories of how different welfare regimes develop and how welfare systems should be classified (Castles, 2009). Social innovation also raises questions about path dependency and historical institutionalism: that is, the extent to which previous actions and investments create a legacy resistant to radical departure, and what circumstances enable systems, organisations or practices to change significantly (David, 1985).

Welfare systems develop distinctive cultures which are embodied in formal institutions and regulations as well as informal customs and beliefs, and these traditions vary across different societies (European Commission, 2013a: 30). Some welfare cultures may be more comfortable and compatible with social innovation than others, creating different environments which stimulate or stifle innovation (Grimm et al, 2013: 447). One commentary on the cultural and institutional receptiveness to social innovation among European Union countries observed patterned variations:

> To classify Member States into broad categories, the *Nordic countries* have been the most open to social innovation as a tool to renew their social model and promote their social and economic performance. Actors in *Anglo-Saxon countries* have also been very proactive following the intense deregulation of the 1980s and the need to rebuild the provision of social services. *Continental countries*, with their heavier institutional traditions, have been less reactive, social innovation often being an add-on which fails to penetrate the system. In *Mediterranean countries*, the persistence of strong systems of informal solidarity has also slowed down the process, and amongst the *eastern Member States*, the weakness of having a civil society with no autonomous organisation or capacity has been a severe handicap. (BEPA, 2010: 10, emphases in original)

Therefore institutional and political opportunity structures in different countries shape the development of social innovation. For example, the German welfare system – usually described as Bismarckian or corporatist – provides somewhat fewer opportunities for social innovations to develop and flourish than more liberal or mixed economies of welfare, and Social Democratic regimes in Scandinavia provide least of all (see Chapter 5) (Ruddat and Schönauer, 2014). As a result, it may be necessary to adapt or finesse how social innovation is presented for it to be to be accommodated within particular national contexts or accepted by some communities (Frane and Westland, 2013).

Social innovations may challenge or even subvert existing practice. While this may produce longer-term benefits, disruption may be perceived as potentially threatening and therefore provoke resistance. It is no surprise that 'Radical ideas that threaten a significant shift in power are likely to face particularly ferocious opposition' (Mulgan et al, 2007a: 13). It is also widely recognised that, generally speaking:

> Once an organization is invented it seldom concerns itself with inventing new ways to deliver its service or objectives. Instead, it becomes consumed with developing methods of self-maintenance and extension ... Therefore, most instrumental social inventions will be expected to be made outside the institutions in which they should be developed and utilized. (Conger, 1996, n.p.)

Change may be resisted if existing institutions are reluctant to jeopardise resources already committed ('sunk costs') (Moore and Westley, 2011: 2). On the other hand, this inertia can benefit social innovations which have secured policy support or endorsement, as the public sector is generally slow to decommission or divest from initiatives which have received considerable political capital or other visible investments (Mulgan et al, 2007a).

Innovation may be inefficient in the short term if it generates friction with existing institutions and systems, diminishes institutional know-how or weakens the networks and social relationships which lubricate how organisations function. As noted in Chapter 1, some public institutions may be uncomfortable with the potential risks involved in collaborating with or relying upon social innovations to deliver welfare services (Caulier-Grice et al, 2012: 28). Public bodies and elected officials who are responsible for statutory entitlements may prefer security and predictability over potentially risky innovation. Social innovations might excel at improving practice through improvisation (although this remains to be seen: see Chapters 3–5), but improvisation may be unnerving for public agencies and service users who depend upon regular and reliable provision. Public welfare agencies may therefore have good reason to be anxious about the capacity of what might be new, small and less experienced social innovations to provide essential services, particularly where potentially catastrophic failures cannot be tolerated (European Commission, 2013a: 17). Therefore, in some cases social innovations and other reforms may be diluted or only partially implemented so that they may be contained by those with an interest in preserving the *status quo* (Conger, 1996).

The potentially fraught relationship between social innovations and existing welfare systems and public institutions is further complicated by the role which political and ideological factors inevitably play in social and public policy. Organisations and institutions responsible for public resources must consider political realities which social innovations might be able to ignore. One such consideration is public opinion. The public might not be informed or even reasonable in its views on some social and public policy issues, but no elected policy maker can ignore popular preferences with impunity. Consequently, some potentially promising social innovations in politically contentious areas (particularly criminal justice, drug user rehabilitation, public health, social protection and employment training) have not been supported by policy makers due to concerns about the risk of negative publicity or public hostility (Mulgan et al, 2007a: 16).

Substantive social innovation questions

As noted above, to be more than interesting local curiosities, social innovations cannot function only at a micro level, but must contribute to substantive improvements in social conditions. Evaluating their capacity in this respect involves considering two dimensions of social innovations: how they function (process issues) and what outcomes they achieve.

The processes of social innovation

Many analyses of social innovation and service co-production focus more on how they function than their effects (Voorberg et al, 2014). This focus is not necessarily misplaced: from the perspective of service users, how a social innovation (or any welfare service) operates is very important (Wright and Haux, 2001). Among the principal operational issues to consider when comparing social innovations to more conventional welfare providers are the following:

- Policy-making and administration processes: how priorities are chosen, actions decided upon and measures delivered.
- Accountability, transparency and opportunities to scrutinise policy-making and implementation processes.
- Treatment of service users: for example, service responsiveness, respect for dignity and potential sensitivities.
- Equality of provision and outcomes (relative to need): are there unjustified or arbitrary variations in provision? Are services distributively just?
- Citizenship rights: do services provide enforceable entitlements with a guaranteed legal foundation, a right to appeal against decisions and redress for poor service quality, etc?

Some advocates of devolved decision making propose that 'policymakers should create more opportunities for communities to develop and deliver their own solutions and to learn from each other' (Bunt and Harris, 2010: 6). While on the face of it this may seem persuasive, there are potential hazards in delegating services to local communities and non-public bodies. The challenge which social innovations face in reconciling innovation and flexibility with reliable and equal provision has been noted. Innovation is not necessarily an improvement if better outcomes are achieved at the expense of accountability or reliability. For all their potential inefficiencies and insensitivities, standardised services have some advantages. For example, relatively few social innovations can provide the institutionalised rights which underpin core areas of public welfare, such as healthcare, education provision or social protection (Evers et al, 2014: 24). While it might seem unreasonable to place such demands upon independent social innovations, this becomes legitimate if social innovations replace or assume the role of public welfare providers, as many supporters of social innovation recommend and as has already happened in some countries.

Social citizenship rights have a juridical foundation; that is, they are entitlements rather than charity. Entitlements 'describe a relationship of persons to commodities by which their access to and control over them is "legitimized". Entitlements give people a rightful claim to things' (Dahrendorf, 1988: 9). In contrast to discretionary and potentially unreliable charity, entitlements are impersonal and legally enforceable. Entitlements are also justiciable; that is, eligible claimants have a right to appeal if due processes have not been followed (Veit-Wilson, 2102). Services based on citizenship rights may also be accessed by claimants without being subject to additional moral tests, such as judgements of their supposed deservingness. These qualities ensure that services provided through conventional public welfare systems are relatively reliable and predictable. The capacity of what may be precariously funded social innovations to match the security of core-funded public provision must therefore be considered.

The impact of social innovation

Some supporters of social innovations and social enterprises claim that they are 'more effective, efficient, sustainable, and just than existing solutions' (Phills et al, 2008), and that they 'have made it possible to provide social and general interest services in a way that is economically sustainable, and in many ways more effective and efficient than what could be done by the public sector alone' (European Commission, 2013a: 32). It was noted in Chapter 1 that the idea that they are more effective and produce 'tangible improvement' is built into some definitions of social innovation (see, for example, Young Foundation, 2012: 12). However impact is an empirical question to be asked of social innovations, not a quality to be assumed *a priori*. Evidence is required to establish whether they provide better outcomes, more cost-effective and efficient responses to social needs or benefits beyond those delivered by conventional public and welfare services. For example, do social innovation initiatives have any distinctive impact in relation to community efficacy or capacity? Empowerment has not traditionally been a notable strength of many conventional social and public policies. In fact, one recurring (but often ignored) lesson of area-based community regeneration initiatives is that positive outcomes are considerably more likely if residents and service users are engaged in designing and implementing reforms (Thornhill, 2009). Therefore, participation and empowerment should be characteristics of all social and public policies, not simply social innovations. One positive contribution which social innovations may have made to debates in social and public policy is to reinforce this point, and affirm the importance of citizen and service users' participation in decision-making.

Beyond their direct effect on services users and communities, particularly important considerations for social and public policy are the sustainability and transferability of practice. While any local benefits produced by innovative initiatives should be applauded, the value of social innovations to social and public policy depends upon their capacity to be scaled up to achieve wider impact, and scaled out and replicated across different settings (Moore and Westley, 2011: 4). Social innovations are often very context-dependent and 'locally or regionally specific' (Moulaert, 2009: 12). Many social innovations are small and lack the staff and resources required to scale up their activities (Caulier-Grice et al, 2012: 27). Relatively few possess the capacity to engage in longer-term strategic planning, least of all during periods of resource constraint (Norman et al, 2013: 13). The organic and grassroots nature of social innovation is both a strength and a potentially significant limitation in terms of effecting significant social change (Seyfang and Smith, 2007). Their 'strong strand of localism ... implies that policy instruments effective in one country may not work in another and the same may be true at regional level' (Grimm et al, 2013: 446; see also Sahlin and Wedlin, 2008). Consequently, there are relatively few social innovations developed in a particular context and through a unique set of relationships and collaborations which have been successfully replicated or transferred to different settings (Caulier-Grice et al, 2012: 40). For example, despite its success in the UK *The Big Issue* (a magazine sold by people experiencing homelessness) failed in the United States due to unfavourable market conditions (Mulgan et al, 2007a).

Case Study: The Big Issue

The Big Issue is a UK street magazine sold by people who are homeless. Since its launch in 1991 it has become one of the most visible social enterprises and a prominent member of the international street newspaper movement. *The Big Issue* provides basic training, an initial supply of magazines (provided on credit) and a vendor's badge to people who are homeless, who commit to a code of conduct when selling the magazine. When vendors have sold their initial allocation of magazines, they can buy additional copies at 40–50% of the cover price and retain the rest of the sales price. *The Big Issue* is based on the principle that earning an income helps empower homeless people in a way that receiving charity does not. It also conveys a more positive impression of those who are homeless to members of the public, who see them working to change their situation.

The Big Issue was inspired by *Street News*, a newspaper sold by homeless people in New York. The original British version received start-up funding from the Body Shop and is now a social enterprise financed through sales and advertising revenue. A separate charitable Big Issue Foundation was established in 1995 to receive additional donations. Any surplus revenue is invested and used to advance the welfare of vendors.

After initially being launched in London, several franchises were established across the UK. *The Big Issue* also participated in the creation of the International Network of Street Papers in 1994 to advise members on how to set up or improve their own street newspapers. The network was initially funded by the European Commission and is now a registered UK charity. Versions of *The Big Issue* have been launched in Australia, South Africa, Namibia, Japan and elsewhere. However, attempts to launch franchises in the US met with mixed success and generated controversy, as some were viewed as competing with existing street newspapers (including *Street News* in New York).

Nevertheless, *The Big Issue* can claim to be one of the most familiar, established and admired social innovations in the UK, with a record of assisting thousands of people who are homeless to improve their lives. It is not a criticism but a recognition of the scope of its reach that homelessness remains an unresolved and increasing problem in the UK, despite its considerable efforts and impact.

This relates to the previous discussion of the varying receptiveness of different welfare regimes and political cultures to social innovation. In particular, significant challenges arise in transferring social innovations developed in lower-income countries to the very different conditions and contexts of higher-income nations with extensive public welfare systems. Mavra (2011: 5) concludes that 'research strongly indicated that there is no one right way to replicate; rather, this depends on the nature, social/environmental goal, legal form and financial model' of each social innovation. However, three general forms of replication are identified:

- social franchising: establishing a contracted subsidiary or authorised branch of an existing social innovation model;
- social licensing: a more flexible agreement where a new social innovation borrows particular operational aspects from an existing social innovation
- collaboration: informal partnerships and resource pooling (Mavra, 2011: 5).

In addition to these deliberate processes, social innovations have also spread and expanded by inspiring emulators to launch their own versions of successful initiatives (Mulgan et al, 2007b: 27).

One characteristic of social in contrast to other forms of innovation is that there may be no incentive or market mechanism which drives activities to be scaled up or out: 'There are no equivalents in social policy to the market mechanisms of Schumpeter's "creative destruction" that leads to new innovations in the private sector wiping out older technologies' (European Commission, 2013a: 14). The WILCO research project found that some social innovations have no interest in operating beyond the context and community they were developed to assist (Evers et al, 2014). Similar parochialism is also evident among some British credit unions, which regard their role as benefiting existing members rather than addressing wider financial exclusion (Sinclair, 2014). Those involved in forming and developing successful social innovations may be anxious about becoming overstretched, maintaining the intimate stakeholder relationships on which their success depends, or risking mission drift if they expand or spread. Some may simply be concerned about losing control of an initiative which they have carefully nurtured and in which they have invested so much (Mulgan et al, 2007a). Growing beyond a certain size also requires social innovations to implement formal structures and control systems. In short, expanding or extending their impact requires social innovations to address the challenges of bureaucratisation which confront any organisation founded on charismatic authority (Gerth and Mills, 1948: 54). These numerous and complex institutional, cultural and political impediments therefore cast doubt on the suggestion that 'The ultimate aim for any innovation is for it to become mainstream' (William-Powlett, 2014: 14).

Limitations to social innovation

Voorberg et al have proposed the following definition of social innovation:

> the creation of long-lasting outcomes that aim to address societal needs by fundamentally changing the relationships, positions and rules between the involved stakeholders, through an open process of participation, exchange and collaboration with relevant stakeholders, including end users, thereby crossing organizational boundaries and jurisdiction. (2014: 1334)

This is a very challenging benchmark which requires social innovations to meet four exacting criteria. There are few initiatives which qualify on all counts. In particular, the requirement that social innovations achieve 'long-lasting outcomes' is demanding, not least because it is difficult to know whether any impacts which may be attributed to social innovations will be sustained over the longer term. Therefore further analytic questions that social innovations raise concern the duration of their effects, what factors and conditions contribute to their success and sustainability, and whether there are particular supporting mechanisms which assist this.

As many supporters of social innovation point out, 'what makes local solutions effective is their local specificity, and the ability of groups to tailor solutions to local contexts' (Bunt and Harris, 2010: 4). Local social innovations may or may not be better at delivering particular services, but it is important to be realistic about their potential impact. Many social problems are caused by macro-structural factors which lie beyond the boundaries of the communities where they appear. Social innovation might improve conditions in some of the sites where problems become evident but leave their macro-structural causes untouched (Lupton, 2003; Alcock, 2005). Even the most vibrant local initiatives cannot protect communities against macro socioeconomic forces. For example, improving the employment skills of particular individuals or groups does not ensure that there are jobs available for them (see Chapter 5). Therefore, while social innovations may ameliorate individual experiences, 'very few social innovations effect or reach the stage of systemic change'; they have limited capacity to transform social conditions (Caulier-Grice et al, 2012: 34).

Consequently, although they may be valuable to and valued by their immediate beneficiaries, it is important to be realistic about the social impact of most social innovations. Few are able to deliver services of general interest, that is, those fundamental to maintaining social wellbeing and quality of life, such as basic infrastructure (for example, energy, clean water and sanitation, transport systems), health, education and social care services (European Commission, 2013b: 21). Providing such essential services is beyond the capacity of most social innovations, although they may be valuable as pilot programmes and provide lessons and sources of insight which could be applied to macro-social policies.

The voluntary, organic and community-based nature of social innovations resembles forms of collective self-provision which predate national welfare states, and also corresponds to aspects of communitarianism (Etzioni, 1995; Sandel, 2010). This quality of social innovation appeals to otherwise diverse advocates in the UK, including David Cameron's much vaunted but short-lived idea of the Big Society, proponents of 'active citizenship' and the Blue Labour movement within the Labour Party (Nosko and Széger, 2013).[2] The voluntary and entrepreneurial nature of social innovation contrasts with most conventional state-funded and state-run public welfare services. Statutory public welfare services may be more secure and generally reliable than social innovation, but they are criticised as infringing individual choice and liberty, and may be subject to greater political interference than civil society social innovations (Artemis and Sawyer, 2004). Societal-wide public welfare policies and systems also depend upon a collective commitment to mutual support. The social and economic transformations outlined in Chapter 1 threaten the social cohesion and sense of shared identity upon which public welfare systems depend. Insecure employment, increased social diversity and fluidity erode the structures of solidarity required to sustain public enthusiasm for collective welfare provision. It is not yet possible to say whether social innovations can fill or repair this eroding sentiment. However, so far none of the alternative social networks and exchange systems which have accompanied, and in some cases been associated with, social innovation (such as the sharing economy) have generated the dense interactions and intense bonds which form strong collective identities. A collective commitment to pool resources to share and spread risks (that is, distributive solidarity) is unlikely to emerge from the limited and fleeting connections of online networks and virtual relationships. These do not provide the structurating conditions required to generate shared identities and sustained collective action (Giddens, 1991). Small community-based social innovations may create such bonds on a local scale, but cannot themselves reshape macro-social conditions. In fact, intense local solidarity might even weaken attachment to wider social identities, thereby undermining support for macro social welfare systems and policies.

Social innovation and social movements

In their analysis of the various strands in the discourse of social innovation, Ayob et al (2016: 11) identify a radical perspective which emphasises the role of social innovations in promoting societal change and restructuring power relations. Macro-social and international examples – such as environmentalism or the European Union – blur the boundary between social innovations and what may be regarded as social movements, and raise the question of what might be the relationship between these ideas.

According to Mulgan et al (2007a: 22) the 'ultimate goal' of scaling up social innovations is to change how societies think. This brings social innovations close to some of the activities of social movements, which agitate for the issues which concern them to be reconceptualised (Spector and Kitsuse, 1987). For example, the disabled rights movement campaigned not only for new policies but also to change the discourse of disability, redefining it as a social and civil rights rather than a medical issue (Shakespeare, 2013). The Civil Rights movement in the United States and social movements in the late nineteenth and early twentieth century – such as the labour movement or campaign for women's suffrage – were overtly revolutionary, in the sense that they sought to transform law, policy, social relations and ideas. Most contemporary social innovations are not political or social movements in this sense; few have 'transformational' aspirations which directly challenge core social institutions and social structures. In many cases they provide alternatives *within* mainstream society and systems which they leave intact. For example, credit unions and microfinance providers do not challenge but rather operate in parallel to and sometimes in partnership with mainstream banking and financial systems. To be considered genuinely disruptive, social innovations would oblige existing actors, institutions and policies to change, just as trade unions and the labour movement compelled change among employers and governments.

Therefore although they possess some of the qualities of a social movement, most social innovations are largely apolitical. They do not consistently organise and press for political change at a national level, and are less a cohesive social movement than a conglomeration of local projects and initiatives. While social innovations may cooperate and pool resources on an ad hoc basis, they are too diverse and dispersed to promote a sustained platform or manifesto and are therefore not an engaged political force. Their political character and role may be closer to what Burke described as the 'little platoons' and affiliations which bond communities together (1790: 39), or what de Tocqueville regarded as the associations of civil society – which contribute to the fabric of democracy (2010: 302ff). Small-scale, bottom-up and unorganised social innovations may accommodate to social structures and adapt to existing power relations rather than challenge them. In this respect, they could be regarded as conservative rather than radical political forces.

Contesting social innovation

'Like every new attractive concept, social innovation holds some risks' (BEPA, 2010: 40). Although there is an emerging consensus over its definition, the social innovation discourse neither prescribes an agreed set of policies nor points to consistent political reforms. However, its dual nature of simultaneously enhancing and disrupting existing social arrangements means that social innovation poses a potential threat to established welfare systems as well as offering new opportunities to enhance social inclusion (Nicholls and Murdock, 2012). This duality has led some commentators to warn that 'social innovations are not necessarily objectively "good" or socially positive' but have a potential 'dark side' (Caulier-Grice et al, 2012: 17) For example, microcredit has been criticised for legitimising a 'neo-liberal narrative which offers individualized solutions to collective and societal injustices' (Grimm et al, 2013: 445).

The discourse of social innovation is therefore both ambiguous and politically contentious. It is one of several concepts with potentially progressive and regressive implications, similar to such ideas as individual and community 'resilience', an 'asset-based approach' to health and wellbeing, 'localism' and 'social capital', to name just a few. Table 2.1 outlines the potential politically 'progressive', structural and left-leaning interpretations of social innovation and alternative potentially conservative, individualistic and 'reactionary' meanings.

Table 2.1: Progressive v conservative interpretations and implications of social innovation

Progressive interpretation and implications	Conservative interpretation and implications
Focus on prevention and salutogenesis, ie social conditions which protect health and promote wellbeing (Lindström and Eriksson, 2005)	Focus on self-reliance and self-help (Smiles, 1996)
Empowering initiatives which cultivate community strength and initiative	The dark side of social capital, eg closure, exclusion, parochialism and reduced social solidarity (Portes and Landolt, 1996)
Publicly engaged localism: developing and supporting responsive and user-led services	Laissez-faire localism: state disengagement and public service withdrawal
Collectively addressing adverse social conditions	Blaming the victim (Ryan, 1971)

Social innovation is not located easily on any conventional left/right political spectrum; nor in fact is it easily located on a straightforward liberal/authoritarian axis.[3] In the US, for example, social innovation is often interpreted as a response to 'state failure' rather than 'market failure', and in particular the alleged deficiencies of public welfare services (Teasdale, 2011: 5; Caulier-Grice et al, 2012: 5). The rhetoric and practice of social innovation can be readily promoted by neoconservative and liberal market ideologies and used to critique public welfare provision. The current prominence of social innovation might therefore be an expression of a loss of faith in the policies and public welfare institutions developed during the 'golden age' of the welfare state (Hobsbawm, 1994: 8).

Concerns have therefore been expressed that social innovation may be advocated as an alternative to rather than a way of augmenting public welfare provision and used 'simply as a way of privatising social services' and cutting public expenditure (BEPA, 2010: 40; Moran, 2014). Certainly, one attraction of social innovation for some governments is that it may be a way to provide sustainable self-financing social and welfare services, which enable them, as the European Commission put it, 'do more with less' (Evers et al, 2014: 24). One possible role and future scenario for the development of social innovation is 'basically delegating to people what states seemed not to be able to afford any longer' (Bonifacio, 2014: 151). This possibility has caused concerns and raised objections about potential 'misunderstood subsidiarity', where 'the higher state and economic power levels tend to "shed" their budgetary and other responsibilities to the lower and especially the local levels' (Moulaert et al, 2005: 1978). In some cases, this is not a misunderstanding but a deliberate strategy to transfer more of the responsibility for care and support from the state to communities, civil society organisations and households (Grimm et al, 2013: 451) (see Chapter 5). The 'do it yourself' ethos which underpins so much of social innovation could lead to formal citizenship rights being replaced by voluntary community provision. This is one reason for the caution and concern frequently expressed about social innovation (Godin, 2015).

Conclusions

The idea that the welfare state is in crisis has a long pedigree (see, for example, Habermas, 1973; O'Connor, 1979; Mishra, 1984). The 1970s and '80s were certainly a time of transition for welfare states across the developed world. However, there are good reasons for believing that recent and continuing social and economic changes are even more dramatic than these earlier episodes. Economies and societies across the world are in the midst of unprecedented social changes and new demands. These changing and challenging conditions are evident in a demographic transition, the fluid dynamics of families and households, and shifting community identities and social solidarity. The changes in these areas and the new social and environmental conditions they create involve profound challenges for welfare services, whether provided through the public, private or third sector. The European Commission has warned that 'The sustainability and adequacy of Europe's health and social security systems as well as social policies in general is at stake' (2013a: 5). But beyond Europe similar pressing questions must be addressed:

- Who will provide care for children and increasing numbers of older people?
- Are public or occupational pension systems sustainable and affordable?
- How can insecurely employed and low-paid workers access affordable housing?
- How can access to essential financial and other services be provided to those regarded as 'unbankable' and unprofitable customers?

New socioeconomic and political settlements are required to meet these needs, but it is not yet evident or agreed what forms these will take. Social innovations may be stopgaps in an interval before a new welfare settlement develops, or hybrids in the midst of a prolonged period of improvisation; or they may become institutionalised and form the basis of some entirely new system of welfare. Welfare systems reflect the particular opportunity structures of their time – that is, the distinctive combination of institutional arrangements, historical precedents and political forces which shape policy options and debates (Kitschelt, 1986). The class-based and national bases of solidarity which underpinned the development of collective public welfare provision in the nineteenth and twentieth centuries have been transformed alongside the structural economic and social changes described above, or in some cases they have disintegrated altogether. It is not clear what identities and ideologies will underpin the reform or formation of the new welfare systems that must emerge to meet current and future challenges.

Different opportunity structures are evident in lower-income countries with less developed systems of state welfare, and social innovation might have a different role there. For example, in developing countries social innovation 'might be seen as a means of bypassing the need for welfare state development', just as mobile telephony created new service and market opportunities (such as mobile banking) in Africa and other areas with less developed land telecommunications infrastructure (Ayob et al, 2015: 14). Similarly, the global spread of faster internet connections, social networking and cooperative and co-production opportunities made possible by digital open source technology creates new possibilities for user-led innovation (Grimm et al, 2013: 441). These developments could accelerate the breakdown of distinctions between service producers and users in the same way that partnerships, hybrids and social innovations are making old divisions between the public, private and third sectors redundant. Social innovation could be part of a movement establishing a new relationship between the individual and service providers – enabling or encouraging more participatory, responsive and respectful ways to deliver services (Bunt and Harris, 2010: 4). But alongside their emancipatory and rejuvenating potential, there is also the possibility that social innovation could be used as a Trojan horse to justify dismantling public welfare services and shift responsibilities for providing care onto civil society organisations and communities which may be ill-equipped to cope with such demands. This is why evidence on the contribution and capacity of social innovations to meet pressing social needs is so compelling. The following chapters present and analyse evidence to advance understanding of how social innovations operate in a range of areas and what impact they are having.

Notes

[1] http://siresearch.eu/social-innovation
[2] www.bluelabour.org
[3] www.politicalcompass.org

THREE

Social innovation and food poverty

Introduction

Addressing household food poverty is a social policy issue in which social innovations are more common in Europe and elsewhere than in the UK. Social innovations in this area range from small, neighbourhood-based, citizen groups offering cooked meals, to organisations managing thousands of kilos of donated food. Civil society responses to undernourishment have often outshone government action. In fact, public sector initiatives which have developed in this field are often attributable to the pioneering work of civil society and citizen-based initiatives. This includes both the political lobbying and the campaigning to inform public opinion of the scale of the problem, which non-government organisations have undertaken.

There are several reasons for the growing prominence of bottom-up social innovations addressing food poverty. First, in several European countries there has been a traditional division between state and civil society responsibility in addressing needs, where the state has protected against particular vulnerabilities through mainstream welfare policies (frequently such protection being conditional upon citizens' employment or history of contributions), while civil society organisations provided assistance for what were perceived or portrayed to be marginal or exceptional risks. In this division, undernourishment was often classified as a residual need; either because it was assumed to be covered by mainstream antipoverty and social protection programmes, or because it was thought to affect very marginal categories of people – defined both numerically and socially – such as the homeless.[1] Civil society organisations were therefore tasked with providing food only to those who fell outside conventional public coverage for various reasons. The importance of Food Stamps in the United States is a notable exception to this division within more affluent societies. However, in other contexts this general lack of public provision created the space and need for social innovation to develop to address food poverty.

A second reason for the burgeoning food poverty sector is that, following the 2008 economic and financial crisis, the scale of food insecurity and undernourishment cannot be regarded as a residual problem in Europe and several other countries. By 2014, 9% of EU citizens were experiencing several forms of material deprivation, and 30% of young people aged 18–24 were at risk of poverty (Eurostat).[2] The economic and social transformations described in Chapter 1 (globalisation, precarious employment, migration patterns and changing household formations) have contributed to an increase in the number and range of those needing support to access adequate and appropriate food. Conventional state-based responses have often failed to satisfactorily address these changing and increasing needs. This failure is due not only to increased, intensified and differentiated demands, but is a result of economic policies prioritising public deficit reduction and budgets cuts over welfare expenditure (O'Hara, 2015). In several high-income countries, including the UK, there has been a substantial decline in social spending as a percentage of GDP (OECD, 2014). Thus, despite its salience, food-related needs have remained largely ignored by public bodies in many developed societies.

Third, social innovation in this area reflects decades (if not centuries) of philanthropy on the part of various social organisations, and also traditions of civic engagement that underpin many democracies. This is particularly significant in younger democracies in Central Eastern Europe, where social movements and civil society organisations emerged in opposition to authoritarian regimes. Some of this experience of organising effectively and efficiently to deal with social problems has been drawn upon to address food insecurity in these countries.

Paradoxically, the number of people suffering malnutrition in high-income countries has increased alongside increases in the amount of food wasted every year. Many of the social innovations discussed in this chapter seeks to reconcile this contradiction by collecting surplus food and redistributing it to those in need. Although they share certain features in terms of origin and development, social innovations addressing food poverty take a variety of different forms. This chapter discusses why and how far social innovations provide sustainable and effective responses to meeting this basic need by focusing on three features:

1. organisational innovation: the capacity of social innovations to develop models to organise food collection and distribution which allows them to meet the nourishment needs of vulnerable people while also strengthening organisational capacity;
2. inter-organisational relations: the capacity of social innovations to reconcile the interests and coordinate the actions of a range of actors, for example, combining the interests of food companies (producers, distributors and retailers) and charities or other civil society organisations;
3. interpersonal innovation: the capacity of social innovations to promote effective relations between volunteers and service users which preserve people's dignity and personal integrity.

Figure 3.1 illustrates these three features.

Figure 3.1: Forms of innovation in relation to food poverty

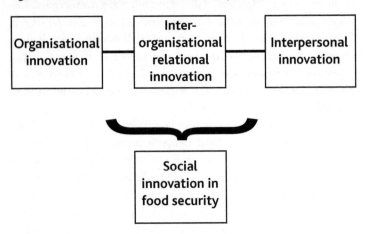

This chapter draws upon a range of evidence, including findings from a research project investigating surplus food recovery policies and practices in four European countries: France, Germany, Italy and Spain.[3] The chapter first provides an overview of food security and food waste issues, then discusses the three recurring features of social innovation highlighted in Figure 3.1 using examples from several European countries. It concludes by providing some reflections on what this evidence suggests about social innovation and social policy.

Food insecurity, surplus and waste

The UN Food and Agriculture Organization defines food insecurity as lacking 'physical, social and economic access to sufficient, safe and nutritious food to meet dietary needs and food preferences for an active and healthy life' (FAO, 2009: 8). Globally, an estimated 800 million people currently experience food insecurity. The problem is not limited to low-income countries; food insecurity is evident in higher-income societies, in part as a result of the economic and financial crisis since 2008, as well as some of the political, social and demographic changes associated with globalisation (IFRC, 2013).

However, in higher-income countries 'food poverty' has traditionally received less attention than other deprivations (Friel and Conlon, 2004). More recently it has become recognised as a salient socioeconomic issue requiring a response from policy makers (Dowler, 1998). Accompanying this growing policy attention, food security has also attracted interest from scholars, as testified to by an expanding literature (Duffy, 2002; Riches, 2002; Gregory, 2005; Engler-Stringer and Berenbaum, 2007; Conceição and Mendoza, 2009; Jha, 2009; Lang and Barling, 2012). The respective academic and policy discourses of food security have both noted a striking contradiction: between the increasing number of people at risk of food poverty and the amount of food daily wasted in production, retail and consumption. While the FAO reports millions of people suffering hunger, at the same time 'roughly one-third of the edible parts of food produced for human consumption gets lost or wasted globally, which is about 1.3 billion ton per year' (FAO, 2011: 4).

While a small amount of surplus food production is unavoidable (Garrone et al, 2014b), food waste is the result of various failures at different stages of the production chain. Food surplus is 'safe food that for various reasons, at any stage of supply chain, is not sold to or consumed by the intended customer' (Garrone et al, 2014b: 1461). This surplus can arise at the post-harvest and processing stages, due to inefficiencies and climate conditions; such is the case in many low-income countries. It can also occur at the retail and consumer stages, due to deficiencies in marketing strategies, product and packaging deterioration or errors in forecasting demand (BCFN, 2012; Garrone et al, 2014a). Beyond the obvious ethical considerations raised by wasting edible food, recovering surplus food has become a key political priority due to the negative environmental impact of food waste. This occurs through its contribution to excess water consumption, depleting environmental resources and generating carbon dioxide equivalent emissions (Baglioni et al, 2016). Given the commercial value of food, waste also has economic consequences (Parfitt et al, 2010; FAO, 2011; Finn, 2011; BCFN, 2012; Ferrara and Missios, 2012; Schneider, 2012; BIO by Deloitte, 2014; Garrone et al, 2014a). The possibility of recovering at least a portion of currently wasted, edible food and redistributing it to those in need has therefore become a core activity for various community-level social innovations. Although this chapter discusses social innovations involved in recovering surplus food, this is not the only way to tackle food poverty in higher-income countries. Nevertheless, it is one model that, combined with other interventions, could address the unmet nutritional needs of some of the most vulnerable sections of society.

Case Study: Food for Soul

Food for Soul is a social innovation which addresses food poverty by involving celebrity chefs in raising awareness of food waste, food vulnerability and the importance of a healthy diet. The project was initiated by the Michelin-starred Italian chef Massimo Bottura, and involves professional chefs preparing meals of the same quality which they serve in their restaurants but using only recovered food. Such meals were provided to homeless people and those experiencing food insecurity during the 2015 Milan International Exhibition in an initiative called 'Feeding the Planet'. This subsequently evolved into Food for Soul, which offers free, quality meals prepared by renowned chefs for socially vulnerable and deprived people. The meals prepared by Food for Soul are provided in a restaurant-style setting to maintain the dignity of those who receive them.

Food for Soul has since become an international non-profit organisation, with branches across Europe (Modena, London, Berlin) and beyond (Los Angeles). Since its inception, 210 celebrity chefs and 600 volunteers have been engaged in the initiative. In 2016 it reported serving more than 16,000 meals, most of which were free, saving 25 tonnes of surplus food from being wasted.

The programme extends beyond preparing and serving restaurant meals: in some locations it also provides premises as community social hubs. In June 2017 it opened a new community kitchen in London, the Refettorio Felix. The initial aim of this latest venture was to provide 2,000 meals using 5 tonnes of recovered food during the month-long London Food Festival, and build upon this to sustain operating capacity in the longer term.

Social innovation through organisational innovation

Social innovation in the field of food poverty, and in particular in food surplus collection and distribution, requires considerable organisational and logistical capacity. The process involves an organisational chain capable of collecting a product, stocking and then dispatching or distributing it to consumers. Moreover, because food is perishable, not only must organisations possess the means to gather and distribute it, they must also maintain the quality of the food at each stage in the process. The sequence of food collection, storage and distribution must occur within a specific timeframe to preserve edibility across each stage; in some cases this requires refrigeration capacity. Developing the necessary logistical and organisational capacity is often the outcome of incremental organisational learning and adaptation. Social innovations in this area may start from simple charitable and loosely organised activities, such as volunteers collecting food from local groceries. However, many of the social innovations with such origins have subsequently attained a level of organisational competence and capacity comparable to established food businesses. Alternatively, some food poverty initiatives are created by public policy, such as the EU programme for deprived people – the Fund for European Aid to the Most Deprived (FEAD) – launched in March 2014, which replaced the Food Distribution programme for the Most Deprived Persons of the Community (MDP).

The first striking innovation observed when analysing social innovations working in the food recovery field is their capacity to differentiate their activities by developing specific competencies and capacities. In particular, social innovations in this area can be split into three types of organisation: logistical, frontline and hybrids (Baglioni et al, 2016). Logistical food poverty organisations are primarily devoted to collecting food from producers and retailers and distributing it to frontline delivery organisations, which then provide food to people in need. Hybrid organisations perform both of these functions. Logistical organisations have developed expertise in the collection and storage of large amounts of food. They can operate either through formal agreements or through ad hoc cooperation with food production or retail operators. Agreements with large food companies require a relationship based on punctual exchanges. This means that a food producer will regularly donate particular types of food to a logistical organisation at specific times, and that organisation then provides frontline agencies with a reliable supply of food for distribution to those in need. Nationwide agreements of this nature are also useful in cases of ad hoc donations of large amounts of surplus food. An effective logistical organisation can rapidly gather and distribute any unexpected and potentially wasteful surplus caused by overproduction. These organisations can dispatch transport and stock food in suitable warehouses where it can be prepared for redistribution by frontline organisations. The latter usually sign an agreement with the logistical organisation regulating all aspects of their cooperation or, in cases of hybrid organisations, they are local branches of the logistical organisation.

Case study: Fondazione Banco Alimentare

Fondazione Banco Alimentare is the largest Italian food bank, currently supporting more than 1.5 million people across Italy through its wide network of 8,103 local and regional branches and associated organisations. In 2015 it distributed more than 88 tonnes of food, supported by more than 1,800 volunteers.[4] The Fondazione has been a social innovation since its inception in 1989. It was established following a meeting between a food business entrepreneur and a group of citizens interested in replicating the model of a Spanish food bank – the Barcelona-based Fundació Banc dels Aliments (Maino et al, 2016: 75). The food entrepreneur initially contributed financial support and committed to donate the company's surplus food. He also persuaded other major food companies (including Barilla, Ferrero, Kellogg's and Kraft), to donate their surpluses (Maino et al, 2016: 76). Over the past 20 years, the foundation has become a key player addressing food poverty at local, national and European levels, and has also fostered social policy innovation and civic engagement. Indeed, the so-called 'Good Samaritan' law recently introduced in Italy (discussed further in this chapter), owes much to its example and efforts.

The collection and storage capacity of logistical food poverty organisations is considered to be an asset by commercial food companies, as it allows them to move surplus food out of their warehouses or off their shelves in a timely fashion. Moreover, in some cases, such as those in France and Germany, logistical organisations with access to local-level food suppliers, such as large groceries or supermarkets, have the capacity to select products considered eligible for donation directly from the shelves. In this way, they perform a valuable 'cleaning' function on behalf of the food company. Effective food logistical organisations have also developed know-how and capacity that is useful for donor companies. The more experienced logistical organisations know how to deal with the administrative procedures and fiscal issues related to food donation, such as health and safety regulations, thereby sparing donors from the need to deal with these.

Frontline organisations have pioneered a variety of innovative forms of food redistribution for those in need. These include quasi-supermarkets or shops offering free food or selling it for nominal prices to a range of eligible customers, for example, those registered by social services as in need of assistance, or those, such as asylum seekers or unemployed people, referred by charities or other agencies. These social innovations have created restaurants or canteens which provide precooked food and ready to eat meals. They have also delivered prepared food bags and meals to those in need.

Many of these organisations work in innovative ways. Most of their work is undertaken by volunteers, often elderly people who are able to apply their professional skills and social knowledge to benefit others. Volunteers carry out most of the work: acting as drivers, food selectors and cooks; shop assistants, accountants and finance specialists; and organisational administrators and managers. Some logistical organisations also have employees, although this is less common among frontline organisations. Volunteers need to be genuinely committed to their duties, as failing to attend a collection or delivery shift or to staff a shop may endanger the work of the entire organisation. In fact, missing a collection appointment could jeopardise the collaboration between the food supplier and the social innovation. Therefore, maintaining the commitment of volunteers is something with which organisations are particularly concerned. As a result, organisations spend considerable time and resources reinforcing volunteers' motivation and engagement, as the principal rewards they receive for their work are moral and social. Volunteers are also essential because they deal directly with service users, and they therefore have to be prepared or coached to interact positively with and treat vulnerable people with due care and professionalism.

Inter-sectoral and organisational partnerships

An essential precondition for social innovations addressing food insecurity is the creation of collaborative relationships between the food production and retail businesses and civil society organisations. These social innovations rely upon companies being willing to donate their surplus food, as civil society organisations would be unable to afford the food they distribute. Many social innovations reinforce this relationship by highlighting how their work benefits food companies. Food donation is therefore presented to companies as a way to contribute to the community wellbeing and fulfil corporate social responsibility duties. It also allows companies to monitor their production capacity and anticipate potential shortcomings; and in several European countries, food donation has become a way to reduce companies' waste bill (Baglioni et al, 2017).

These partnerships between private sector and not-for-profit actors function due to the relationships of trust which have been established across sectors. Trust plays a pivotal role in this, as it serves to overcome risks which would otherwise make food donation too hazardous. Two particular risks which food companies must minimise are: (i) that the food they donate is not misused (for example, sold in informal markets); (ii) that the food they donate is not mistreated, does not violate health and safety regulations, and will not potentially harm consumers. The potential commercial and reputational damage these risks entail would override any benefits which companies derive from donation. Establishing formal, legally binding agreements between social innovations and food companies to minimise these risks is primarily a cautionary procedure that occurs only *after* mutual trust has already developed. Trust in this case flows in two directions. On the one side, social innovations trust that food suppliers will donate a regular and reliable supply of good quality, edible food. In return, food companies trust social innovations not to sell donated products to potential competitors and to ensure it does not pose any health risk to consumers.

Such reciprocal trust-based expectations develop over time through each partner successively meeting the other's expectations. This relies upon social innovation volunteers dealing effectively with food suppliers. Often this involves volunteer drivers collaborating with food suppliers, such as independent grocers or the general manager of a supermarket. On the part of the food industry, this trust depends upon the willingness and behaviour of managers in charge of donations. The interpersonal ties and trusting relationships that underpin these social innovations are created and reinforced by weekly meetings and discussions, leading to systematic, long-term mutual help.

Interpersonal innovation: valuing people

A third dimension of innovation characteristic of action in this field relates to the effect upon service users as well as upon those (such as volunteers) involved in these programmes. This is significant, given the importance of enhancing social relationships and empowering participants in theoretical analyses of social innovation.

Those receiving food donations clearly benefit by having a pressing and essential need met. However, many social innovations also make an effort to dispense this aid in ways which resemble conventional food purchasing and consumption activities. One way in which they do this is to replicate as best they can the layout of supermarkets and conventional shopping experiences, even though their customers either pay only a nominal price or receive products for free. These measures are intended to help the people they support to retain or regain some experience of ordinary life rather than feel embarrassed by their reliance on charity.

In addition to the core function of meeting basic food requirements, many of these social innovations also provide their clients with spaces and opportunities for socialising, such as a meeting area or cafe. This enables service users to spend time interacting informally, as they would in a conventional retail or leisure space. In the difficult and often isolating circumstances in which many of the service users find themselves (such as being immigrants or asylum seekers in a new country, unemployed, or elderly people with no family connections) this opportunity to socialise with people may be as valuable as receiving food. The attention devoted to recreating 'ordinary life' for people who are often confronted with extraordinary challenges reflects the consideration many of these social innovations give to preserving service users' dignity. Such respect is also manifest in the care with which volunteers screen the food placed on shelves or included in food bags. As one charity manager of a donation-based food store in Germany interviewed for the Foodsaving project put it, "We want to avoid our customers thinking that because it's free food we give them it is 'second rate' or scrap products."[5] The dignity of service users is also preserved by offering a variety of food which meets particular dietary requirements and/or is compatible with different religious beliefs.

These social innovations provide volunteers with opportunities to perform useful social functions, enabling them to retain a sense of value, purpose and social connection. Many of these volunteers are older people, students or unemployed; devoting their time and commitment to these social innovations enhances their own dignity and self-respect, as it affords them an opportunity to apply their professional and practical skills and contribute to meeting social needs.

Social innovation and policy impact

The social innovations addressing food poverty discussed here are the outcome of partnerships among a constellation of actors, each playing different functions and roles. Figure 3.2 summarises the principal governance relationships involved in recovering surplus food to address food poverty. At the top are food companies donating products. These donors use the capacities of civil society organisations that perform the various functions involved in collecting and storing large volumes of food for distribution to the frontline agencies that deliver it to people in need. Food donors and collectors require the support and agreement of public authorities which set tax, food hygiene and safety, waste disposal and other regulations. Such regulations are a potential obstruction to food collection and donation. Therefore effective dialogue and collaboration is required between the various actors in the food donation and supply chain and public authorities.

Across Europe, this dialogue has generated a range of recent policy innovations aimed at enhancing the capacities of businesses and social operators involved in surplus food recovery and distribution. Although the donation of surplus food is seemingly a matter of consensus, it depends on a supportive policy and regulatory environment. For example, in many countries it is more convenient for food companies to dispose of surplus food through composting or as waste rather than donating it to food banks. Introducing fiscal incentives and tax benefits to companies donating food are obvious ways to encourage and increase donations. Such measures have been adopted in several European countries. These concessions and forms of financial support are examples of 'corporate welfare' (Farnsworth, 2004, 2012).

Donations may be hindered by the health risks associated with food perishability. Companies may suffer from any cases where food which they have donated has not been properly preserved and poses a hazard. Legislation removing such liability from businesses has encouraged donation. The extension of such legislation to remove responsibility from charities has further strengthened the food supply and distribution chain. This is one of the intentions of the so-called 'Good Samaritan Law' recently introduced in Italy, following the example of the US (Baglioni et al, 2017).

Social innovation in food surplus recovery and distribution has had a further impact on policy innovation in France, where policy has moved beyond moral exhortation and incentives to compulsion, as legislation introduced in 2016 made donation of surplus food an obligation for large retailers. In this case, French civil society organisations and social movements have, in partnership with the food industry, successfully altered the policy context to support and facilitate their social innovation.

Figure 3.2: Governance relations in the food poverty sector

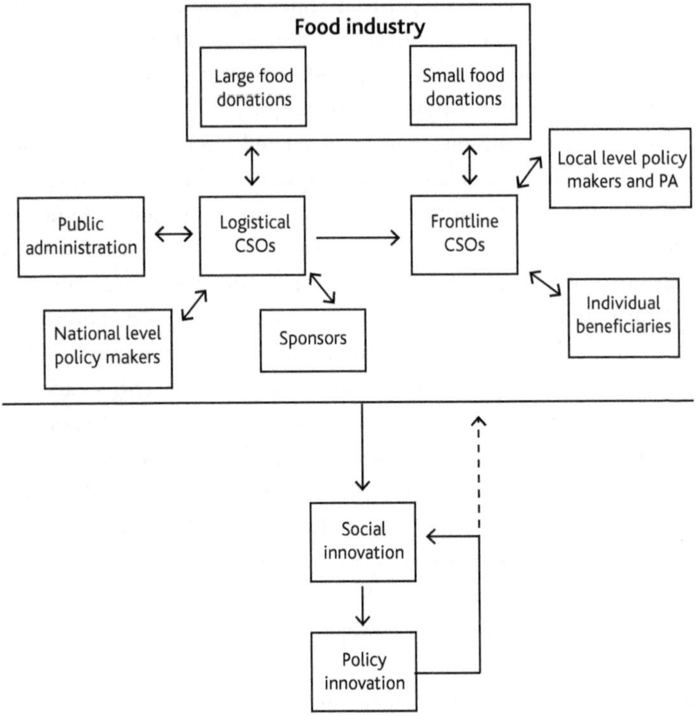

Conclusions

Food poverty has become a policy concern in many higher-income countries, as global political and socioeconomic changes in employment, households and population structures have challenged the wellbeing of large sections of the population. In many such countries there is no tradition of large-scale public action to address food security, as undernourishment was previously considered a marginal problem which was addressed by general welfare policies or private philanthropy. However, more recently there has been much greater civil society activity in developing responses to address unmet nutritional needs and to call for more effective public policy responses. Starting from the seemingly simple idea of collecting surplus food and redistributing it to those in need, social innovations have generated a plethora of innovative partnership with private companies, ranging from local to national programmes. These social innovations have not only aimed at meeting food and related needs, they have also supported the social integration of people in very challenging circumstances, such as the long-term unemployed, low-income households, homeless people, asylum seekers, refugees and migrants.

These social innovations have been made possible by three related innovations. First, the innovation of CSOs developing models and systems to collect and distribute surplus food. Second, policy innovation produced by inter-sectoral cooperation between actors with different aims and ideas, in particular, partnerships between food companies, not-for-profit civil society organisations and public authorities. Finally, CSOs have been innovative in how they deal with service users to protect their dignity and personal integrity. This chain of innovations has led in turn to various policy reforms. These include significant policy innovations, such as the case of France, which introduced a legal obligation to donate surplus food. Milder reforms include measures to support surplus food donation by refining fiscal or tax liabilities, waste disposal and health and safety regulations, and conditions relating to volunteering.

These social innovations address needs not met by existing public provision. Consequently, it is not possible to assess whether they offer more responsive and/or cost-effective provision than statutory or conventional services. The quality of their provision generally seems high, but a more fundamental fact is that they exist at all, addressing a need where public provision is absent or inadequate. In addition, these social innovations reach populations who, in many cases, are not full citizens, either legally (as in the case of asylum seekers) or because they may be described as suffering the partial citizenship of social exclusion. In this respect, these social innovations expand the boundaries of welfare and citizenship. Hunger and undernourishment are basic deprivations and reducing such destitution is clearly a benefit that these social innovations provide. However, beyond meeting such essential needs and fulfilling a fundamental human right, these social innovations also benefit and empower both users and volunteers by offering care, expressing solidarity, and providing them with opportunities for social interaction and engagement (Garthwaite, 2016). Many of these social innovations cooperate closely with public welfare institutions. For example, many of those who receive food from social innovations are referred to them by public authorities. Social innovations also receive public support through the provision of grants and subsidised premises, and have benefitted from regulatory or legislative reforms designed to increase corporate food donations or ease the distribution and supply processes.

Although there have been recent policy developments to address food poverty in several countries, in the absence of adequate public action these social innovations – developed by constellations of actors from the third and private sectors – have been the main source of support and relief to people in need of essential food. This relief also offers opportunities for social integration and therefore perhaps partial reconstruction of a social fabric worn thin, if not torn to shreds, by disruptive economic and social transformations. Such sociability and repair may be one distinctive contribution of social innovation; it is certainly a precondition for enhancing social cohesion and wellbeing.

Case Study: MyFoody app

MyFoody is a social innovation which uses technology to reduce food waste. MyFoody is a smartphone app which alerts customers when a shop has food which will shortly expire, or products with damaged packaging, which are available for sale at discount prices (reduced by up to 50%). This benefits both customers and businesses. Customers are attracted by cheaper prices, improve their awareness of food waste, and are encouraged to adopt more efficient and ethical purchasing practices. Food retailers reduce their food waste (and corresponding waste disposal bills), attract new customers and strengthen customer loyalty; they may also rebrand themselves as ethical and responsible businesses.

MyFoody also provides customers with the option of donating any savings they have made by using the app to a range of charities, social enterprises or philanthropic activities.

Notes

[1] In Europe public action in relation to food has primarily focused on reducing overeating and obesity, regarded as a policy priority because of the effect on public health and associated budget costs.

[2] 'People at risk of poverty', http://ec.europa.eu/eurostat/statistics-explained/index.php/People_at_risk_of_poverty_or_social_exclusion

[3] The project was entitled 'Foodsaving: at the Crossroad of Social Innovation', and funded by the Fondazione Cariplo and the Government of the Lombardy Region (for further information see www.foodsavingproject.it).

[4] http://www.bancoalimentare.it

[5] Interview with German food security charity, 2014.

FOUR

Social innovation and care provision

Social innovations which provide care to vulnerable groups have developed in diverse settings in many countries, as communities, public officials and social entrepreneurs have attempted to develop creative responses to address a variety of underserved or unmet needs (Ewert and Evers, 2014). Because of the complex issues and conditions with which it deals, the care sector is particularly challenged by any gap between increasing and diversifying needs and limited public policy capacity. As a result, this is an area where social innovation has been especially vibrant and imaginative. Social innovations have been developed to help integrate migrants into host societies, to support parents to combine employment and family responsibilities (particularly the childcare requirements of lone parent households), and to facilitate independent living for people with disabilities, as well as in several other areas. As with most of the innovations discussed in this book, social innovations delivering care have a variety of origins and development paths. Some have been created by community or other civil society groups in response to specific issues, while others are the product of the combined effort of public and private sector organisations, often led by local authorities. In several cases, social innovations in this area are the outcome of the enterprise and/or frustration of public officials and local service professionals, who feel compelled to innovate to improve responses to what they regard as urgent or ill-served social needs.

Social innovations providing care are local phenomena, in so far as the issues and needs they address are manifest within neighbourhoods or communities, and this also is the level at which responses are usually developed. While mainstream welfare services set the broad policy context, it is the local and everyday practice of welfare that creates the space for innovation. Social innovations emerge in such spaces as citizen groups and civil society associations, and where local authority officials use what are often quite small amounts of funding to exchange ideas and cooperate to develop initiatives aimed at meeting basic care needs and enhancing collective welfare. Although EU grants and other public funding sources may provide seedcorn support, innovation flourishes in these niches largely in the absence of public provision and institutions. In this sense, social innovation develops and is driven in response to the lack of conventional provision. However, in some cases public policy actors are aware of these gaps and have initiated their own innovations to address them. These provision gaps and niches have prompted and enable a cycle of innovation which in many areas has reshaped local welfare provision.

This chapter examines examples of local care sector social innovations and considers whether such initiatives improve living conditions, provide better services than conventional public provision (where it exists) or empower service users. It starts by considering childcare initiatives aimed at supporting lone parents. It then looks at examples of social innovations supporting migrant integration, and finishes by examining social innovations which support independent living for disabled people, and other models of community living and supported accommodation to which this has given rise. It concludes by reflecting on what these cases imply for social and public policy.

Supporting lone parents and families with children

One of the social changes to which social innovations have had to respond is the increased diversity of families and households. This includes the growing number of lone parent families, which now make up 16% of all households in the European Union (data refer to 2011 – Eurostat, 2015a). The highest proportions of lone parent households are in Latvia and some urban areas in the UK (specifically Belfast, Liverpool, Glasgow and inner London). There are also relatively high rates of lone parenthood in Lithuania, Hungary, Poland and Slovenia. In contrast, there are relatively few lone parent households in the Netherlands and Cyprus, and in particular regions of Belgium, Denmark, Germany, France, Finland and Sweden (Eurostat, 2015a). This increase in lone parent households across Europe is the outcome of a variety of far-reaching social, demographic and economic changes, including new ideas about gender relations and parenting, women's education and employment opportunities, and divorce reform (crude divorce rates have increased by 150% in the European Union since 1965 – Eurostat, 2015a). Most of these single parents are lone mothers – constituting 13.4% of that 16% of households. Many of the social innovations developed in this area address their particular needs. For example, younger lone mothers face particular challenges in combining caring for children with employment or searching for a suitable job in unfavourable and often discriminatory labour markets. This is especially the case in countries with limited parental-support policies (Stier et al, 2001; Ferrera 2008). Some social innovations have sought to address this issue in imaginative ways by addressing the overlapping demands of (single) parenthood and employment.

One such initiative is in the French city of Nantes, where the municipality introduced the principle that public services providing childcare and job placement or employment support should cooperate to enable lone parents (and in particular lower-income mothers) to re-enter the labour market and/or retain their jobs. To implement this principle, the local authority has created 'childhood coordination centres' in areas with the highest concentrations of lower-income lone parent households (Coqblin and Fraisse, 2014). These centres enable childcare and employment support services to coordinate to meet the needs of lone parents. For example, in the event of an emergency, or where a sudden and unexpected need arises, lone parents can access childcare support without having to complete time-consuming application procedures. This programme also provides free or subsidised childminders who are able to advise lone parents and support them with childcare. Employment support and job placement services are also made aware when a client is a lone parent so that they can provide ad hoc guidance and appropriate placement opportunities.

This policy has generated some controversy. In particular, the involvement of childcare services in employment programmes has been criticised, due to concerns that it may shift the focus of childcare services from the wellbeing of children to the economic status of their parents. Critics have also noted that the programme requires childcare staff to possess employment mentoring skills and other knowledge which some may not have. It also burdens them with the responsibility to help parents find a job, which in some cases may increase stress within families rather than enhance their wellbeing (Coqblin and Fraisse, 2014). Nevertheless, this is an example of a local initiative which connects previously separate policy activities and coordinates institutional responsibilities. It is also an innovation which seeks to empower lower-income lone parents who face particular barriers to employment. The initiative has been developed by and within public institutions, and illustrates the intrepreneurial capacity which some care professionals and public sector staff possess, given the opportunity to use this capacity.

A second social innovation addressing some of the challenges of parenthood is in the French city of Lille. This initiative helps families to improve the quality of the time they spend with their children, and enhance children's early development and education. Unlike the case of childhood coordination centres, which is a local authority initiative created by a small number of public officials, the Potes en Ciel project is largely community-led. *Potes en ciel* means literally 'friends in the sky', but the pronunciation also evokes the French word for 'potential'. The initiative is a cafe for children and families, founded in 2006 by a small group of volunteers, to create a space where parents could spend time with their children and other families to undertake creative activities. In addition to being somewhere for families to socialise, the cafe provides innovative educational and extracurricular activities led by parents (Coqblin and Fraisse, 2014). The cafe's opening hours accommodate the needs of parents and include weekends. The facility is particularly appreciated by families with children who are new to the neighbourhood and who have not yet developed local connections and social networks. Lone parents have also welcomed the opportunities that the cafe provides for their children to play, learn and socialise. The popularity of the café is shown by the increase to 356 members and more than 4,000 users in 2012 (Fraisse, 2014).

The cafe is managed entirely by volunteers, which generates community engagement and mutual support among residents. However, this reliance upon volunteers has also been criticised, as it means that the cafe depends upon their commitment and availability, which makes this social innovation potentially vulnerable to the many competing demands to which parents are subject.

Case study: Parler Bambin

As Chapter 1 pointed out, some social innovations are generated and developed, delivered and funded entirely within public institutions. One interesting example of this area is the Parler Bambin ('Toddler talk') initiative in the French city of Lille (Fraisse, 2014). This initiative aims to enhance the contribution which childcare services make to improving the linguistic skills of children from disadvantaged and immigrant backgrounds, in order to reduce social exclusion and educational inequalities.

The programme draws upon techniques developed by linguistic experts and pedagogical research to enhance children's language proficiency. Among the techniques involved are requiring childcare professionals to address children individually rather than as a group, to ask open-ended questions rather than questions which already include answers, and to use pictures rather than reading when teaching children new words. The approach depends upon support and collaboration from the children's families, who are encouraged to adopt these techniques at home. This initiative therefore engages parents and families in their children's education and intellectual development, thereby empowering both adults and children from disadvantaged groups, as well as improving overall educational outcomes.

The programme has been criticised for the risk it involves of labelling children from lower-income households and minority ethnic communities as needing additional help, and its potential to be used as an early detection system to target particular groups. Nevertheless, it has become a popular innovation in education and childcare, and has been reproduced across several areas of France (Fraisse, 2014).

Integrating migrants

Integrating newly arrived migrants into their host country has been another important area of social innovation activity in recent years. Unsurprisingly, such initiatives have been pioneered and developed most often in those countries with the highest levels of migration, such as Germany, in which 8.7 million non-nationals lived on 1 January 2016 (Eurostat, 2017). Much of this activity has focused on promoting the social and labour market integration of migrants. One such social innovation is the Neighbourhood Mothers project in the Friedrichshain-Kreuzberg district of Berlin, mentioned in Chapter 1 (Ewert and Evers, 2014). This project is designed specifically to address the needs of hard-to-reach immigrant households which are especially vulnerable to social exclusion.

The project is funded jointly by the European Social Fund and the local authority, and delivered by an established welfare charity, the Diakonie group. The initiative employs women from immigrant communities (the 'neighbourhood mothers') who are trained to act as outreach and contact points for new immigrants. These 'mothers' liaise between public agencies and immigrants in need of but unfamiliar with social and welfare services. The 'mothers' are selected by two managers from the welfare association in charge of the programme (Diakonisches Werk), who also act as mentors. Each recruit undertakes six months of training on such issues as child development, the transition from kindergarten to formal education, health promotion and nutrition, and citizenship rights (Ewert and Evers 2014). The 'mothers' are equipped and supported to help and advise immigrant families on a range of issues, such as the German childcare and educational systems, and also to respond to problems such as addiction and abuse. This training course also helps to build a team spirit among the 'mothers', and establishes trust and effective working relationships between them and relevant public and private sector agencies.

The innovation of this service is that it involves the extension and diversification of welfare services through peer contact and by drawing upon and contributing to social capital and solidarity. The 'neighbourhood mothers' have direct personal experience of the kinds of issues which new migrants face, and this expertise allows them to act as intermediaries who can break through what would be impenetrable barriers for formal public services. The initiative also has an empowering effect, not least on the 'mothers', who receiving training, are able to earn an income and create community relationships beyond the capacity of more conventional service providers, and whose unique practical expertise and know-how is recognised as valuable. The programme also benefits recipients, as it helps them navigate the complex web of policies and unfamiliar cultures and customs required to participate fully in society. This particular social innovation is also interesting as it involves inter-sectoral collaboration between multiple actors: a welfare association, individual citizens, and communities and local authorities have cooperated to create a hybrid service rather than merely extend conventional practice and provision. These agencies have worked together to overcome social boundaries and barriers and address unmet essential needs to extend the scope of citizenship to vulnerable and potentially marginalised groups.

Supporting independent and mutual living

Although independent living has been recognised as a right of disabled people since the 2006 UN Convention on the Rights of Persons with Disabilities, relatively few disabled people in Europe have the opportunity to exercise that right. Various social experiments have been developed to address this issue. One example is the *condomini solidali* ('solidarity condominiums') in the Italian city of Bologna. The idea behind this initiative was derived from co-housing experiments in Nordic countries in the 1980s and the *gruppi appartamento* programme pioneered in the Emilia Romagna region of Italy about the same time. *Gruppi appartamento* involved several people with learning disabilities sharing accommodation in a condominium supported by social workers or carers. These models have been developed by charities working in partnership with the local municipality to provide sheltered and supported accommodation designed to allow people with disabilities to live independently. This accommodation is adapted to be disabled accessible and made affordable through rent control. Residents are able to live alone or in partnerships, supported by a carer who lives in a separate but neighbouring apartment.

The Bologna municipality has developed a variety of *condomini solidali* for different groups and forms of mutual support. For example, one idea was to house elderly people alongside newly arrived immigrant families. The idea was that the older resident could perform a de facto 'granny' role and assist new immigrants who often do not have family support networks (Faranda, 2013). As mentioned in Chapter 1, another *condominio solidale* model placed elderly people together with university students, with the idea that their respective needs (for company, care and accommodation) would generate mutual support. A different model aimed at increasing job opportunities and improving the flow of labour market information by creating a social enterprise that employed some residents to provide care support to others (Faranda, 2013).

These experiments met with varied levels of success. Bringing together older people and young immigrant families proved problematic, as their needs and habits were often too incompatible to be harmonious. In such cases, the municipality had to appoint an intercultural facilitator to make the experiment viable (Faranda, 2013). However, the condominium accommodating people with disabilities was more successful in supporting independent living. Although some residents criticised the quality, professional standard and consistency of care support, most residents nevertheless considered the experience as a whole to be positive. It allowed many young disabled people in particular an opportunity to move out of their family home and live autonomously in their own affordable and accessible home, and to enjoy a more independent adult lifestyle. What these respective examples show is that to be successful and embraced by users, social innovations have to be embedded in the preferences and lived experiences of those they are intended to benefit.

These social innovations were the result of cooperation between local authorities, professional care providers and citizens, who together expanded the scope and form of welfare provision. Subsequent assessments found that these initiatives would be improved by adopting more considered and appropriate admission criteria, providing more professional and consistent care support, and developing residents' appreciation of the individual and collective benefits of mutual support (Faranda, 2013). These lessons suggest that there may be limits or drawbacks to the spontaneous and organic development of practice which characterises many social innovations. While 'learning by doing' may generate new operating models and innovative techniques, it can also lead to potentially costly mistakes, and therefore must be tempered by reflection and timely adaptation to emerging experiences.

As a final point, it is worth noting that a condition of access to the *condomini solidali* was that applicants signed a formal commitment to provide mutual support. However, the support that residents actually provided to one another was largely informal and arose from everyday interactions and shared experiences. Reciprocity and solidarity were not enforced but developed naturally, and such social bonds may be an asset which social innovations are particularly good at cultivating.

Case study: L'Insolite Fabriq

L'Insolite Fabriq ('the Unusual Factory') is a social innovation addressing attitudes towards disability and employment opportunities for people with disabilities in France. The Factory is a company of professional comedians with disabilities which addresses issues of disability and employment by producing and performing humorous educational plays. The initiative contributes to raising awareness of prejudice against and the stigma often attached to disabled people, which prevent them securing fulfilling and sustainable employment.

The company was formed in 2013 in Lyon by a professional comedian who thought that better use could be made of the neglected acting talent of many performers with disabilities. She recruited nine comedians with a range of disabilities to form a professional theatre group which could represent and depict some of the experiences of people with disabilities in entertaining and stimulating ways. The troupe now has a repertory of several plays, and is hired by private companies and public bodies seeking to educate staff and citizens about disability in an engaging and memorable way. L'Insolite Fabriq therefore conveys the experiences of people with disabilities and challenges some of the prejudices they face through art and performance, in a way which empowers and is led by disabled people themselves.

Conclusion

Judging the quality of innovative experiments in social and public policy is never a simple task, as such initiatives often have multiple objectives and address complex needs. Nevertheless, it does seem that some social innovations in the care sector have succeeded in providing more responsive and appropriate services than conventional public provision, at least for specific groups in particular circumstances. As use of some of these services is voluntary (and in some cases – for example, Potes en Ciel – service users and providers are one and the same) they empower users and enable them to exercise choice and agency. In some cases social innovations have provided forms of care which were simply not provided by mainstream public or private welfare. However, it also seems apparent that the most effective social innovations in this area collaborate or coordinate with conventional welfare institutions and policies, and complement and strengthen rather than challenge these.

In terms of citizenship rights, these social innovations are ambiguous. On the one hand, by providing services where none previously existed, or addressing the needs of unserved or socially marginalised groups (some of whom may not be full legal citizens), they enlarge the scope of welfare provision. However, on the other hand, to the extent that they are improvised or volunteer-led initiatives, these social innovations are often more precarious than guaranteed and fully institutionalised welfare services. These social innovations may spread the benefits of care, but they are less able to consolidate these benefits as rights. Vulnerable people may rely upon them, but their reliability is questionable.

Another striking and recurring feature of many social innovations in this area is how they benefit those who deliver them. For example, the beneficiaries of the Neighborhood Mothers programme are not only the new migrants who are supported to access services and deal effectively with the challenges thrown up by an unfamiliar society. The 'mothers' themselves acquire qualifications, earn an income, enhance their status and improve their individual and community efficacy. At the heart of the most effective social innovations in this area is a degree of mutualism and reciprocity, whether this be an effect of design (as in the condominio solidale cases) or an accident. The most successful of these social innovations therefore transcend established divisions between service producers and consumers.

Most of the social innovations considered here have been developed in partnership with or with the support of existing public welfare institutions and systems, and there are few signs of friction and conflict. In some cases this is because the social innovations have accommodated to the opportunities and demands of the existing institutional infrastructure and policy landscape. In effect, they would not exist at all, or in the form that they do, were they incompatible with their environments. This relates to the question of the potential transferability of some of these models beyond their original settings and cultural contexts. As they are moulded by and adapt to their specific sociodemographic conditions and policy environments, these contexts are integral to their identity. Therefore in one sense they cannot be copied or transplanted beyond the original contexts of which they are part. However, these social innovations offer models, templates and lessons which may be adapted and applied in other circumstances. People with disabilities across the world require and demand supported independent living, and meeting this need through some form of assisted shared accommodation is something which can realistically be developed in a range of different settings. There would be a potential benefit in comparing what can be learned from these different models, and social and public policy analysis could perform a valuable role in identifying and sharing this knowledge.

Some of the social innovations developed to provide care have shown considerable imagination, enterprise and resilience. They offer lessons and models for how welfare can be provided which may be better suited to and more able to meet the challenges of delivering care and enhancing capabilities in the increasingly complex, dynamic and diverse societies of the twenty-first century.

Case study: ESDES Inter-Générations

ESDES Inter-Générations in Lyon is a social innovation which helps elderly people to live independently in their own home in exchange for sharing their residence with a young person. In this way, the initiative simultaneously addresses the needs of different generations: providing university students with accommodation, while also meeting older people's needs for care and social engagement.

Potential elderly hosts are selected through referrals from local public and health services and general advertising. Prospective student guests are recruited through adverts and publicity campaigns at the Catholic University of Lyon and other local universities. Staff at ESDES Inter-Générations screen applicants carefully to ensure an appropriate match between elderly hosts and their young guests. Following this, participants sign a formal agreement which ESDES Inter-Générations monitors through monthly meetings. The student commits to provide company for and share at least one meal per day with their host, and to contribute to basic domestic tasks. Guests are not expected to act as carers; in fact, hosts must be capable of independent living to be selected for the scheme. The service is funded by an annual fee of €300 paid by beneficiaries and by earnings accrued from delivering similar services to public bodies.

ESDES Inter-Générations and similar social innovations have several potential benefits which are not currently provided by existing public or private services. It offers basic care and social engagement opportunities for older people who might otherwise feel isolated and neglected. This enables them to continue to live independent and more fulfilled lives, which are important factors in maintaining health and wellbeing in later life. It also empowers older participants, by enabling them to contribute to the housing needs and social development of their young guests. In turn, students participating in the initiative are not only able to access affordable (and eventually free) accommodation, they also benefit from social engagement, and acquire experience which helps them to develop relational and emotional skills of potential value to their future employment and social relationships.

FIVE

Social innovation and employment

Introduction

As Chapter 3 showed, in societies with highly developed welfare systems, social innovations addressing food poverty have emerged in response to limited public policy provision. In Europe food security has become a salient policy issue only in the last decade, particularly since 2008 and subsequent economic and financial crises. In contrast, there is a much longer tradition of policy addressing unemployment and underemployment. In this field, social innovation has emerged either as a consequence of or a complement to extensive public policy activity. However, recent fiscal and economic crises have exacerbated what was already a key policy concern: the economic situation of young people, who have been particularly vulnerable to unemployment in many European countries. In response to these chronic and acute conditions, policy makers from the local to European Union levels of government have developed a variety of responses. These are often delivered by civil society organisations and/or social enterprises, or as joint ventures between public and private (both for-profit and not-for-profit) sector organisations. The promotion of such civil society-based responses constitutes a policy paradigm shift, in which responsibility for employment has moved from the state to the individual (and, to a lesser extent, the market) (Jessop, 1994; Montgomery et al, 2017). This post-Fordist turn in employment policy has often emphasised individual failings rather than industrial or macroeconomic conditions to account for persistently high unemployment rates. Consequently, policy discourses have focused on strengthening the 'employability' of unemployed people – that is, their skills and knowledge (Peck and Theodore, 2000; Cremin, 2010) – as an essential condition for them to successfully enter, and remain in, the labour market, rather than increasing local labour market opportunities (Baglioni et al, 2008). Alongside this policy shift is the need to address issues which lie beyond the capacity of previous measures and institutions. This incapacity is the result of a combination of new demands (such as those described in Chapter 1, for example, new household forms, population ageing, migration etc) and the limited public resources which many governments either believe are or have made available for policy.

This combination of shifting responsibility and limited room for manoeuvre for public action to meet new needs has created new opportunities for social innovation to become more involved in employment policy. However, within this general policy paradigm, the diverse conditions and contexts of Western societies mean that social innovations have taken various different forms and development paths. To understand these alternative paths, it is first necessary to consider the key features of the European labour market, and in particular the employment situation of younger people.

Case study: Bollenti Spiriti

Developed in a context of high youth unemployment, and a relatively weak economic and industrial infrastructure, Bollenti Spiriti is an example of a publicly led social innovation promoting youth entrepreneurship and creativity in Apulia, Southern Italy. The name translates as 'hot-blooded spirits' – referring to the vibrant, creative spirit of young people.

This initiative pools resources from local, national and European urban and economic development programmes, to fund an innovative approach to developing and supporting employment among young people. A particular innovation of Bollenti Spiriti is that it has created a distinct youth empowerment strategy which operates across a range of what are often distinct and disparate policy areas: culture, industrial development, urban regeneration and environmental measures. The programme operates in five areas:

1. urban regeneration: converting unused public buildings and local authority properties into activity spaces for young people;
2. providing funding of up to €25,000 for projects proposed by young people from the Apulia region;
3. initiatives which promote respect for the rule of law and which counteract the influence of the local mafia;
4. training which strengthens young peoples' local entrepreneurial capacities;
5. education which links young people to job opportunities in local development activities and community support services.

The programme involves collaboration between local government, employers' organisations, social enterprises and cooperatives, charities and a local university. To date, €54 million of public investment has been used to renovate 151 urban centres, which operate as employment and urban regeneration hubs.

Labour market and employment contexts of social innovation

Youth unemployment in Europe is not a new phenomenon; nor is it attributable to the 2008 economic and financial crisis. Nevertheless, over the past 15 or so years European Union member states have failed to create sufficient jobs for young people. Despite a range of policy approaches and strategies, the overall employment situation in the EU has shown little improvement: the average EU unemployment rate never fell below 15% throughout the period 2000–15. The apparent indifference of the European labour market to younger people is a longstanding feature which is far from being resolved. For example, in January 2016, of the over 21 million unemployed people in the EU, 4.4 million were aged between 14 and 24 (Eurostat).[1]

For young people, employment has not only become more difficult to find compared with previous generations, its nature has also changed. Many in their parents' generation had experienced a lifelong, single occupation, regulated through a standard open-ended contract, with legally secure social benefits and often a guaranteed index-linked pension. In contrast, current younger generations will in all likelihood shift between several jobs over their working lives. Furthermore, many of these jobs will be non-standard (fixed-term contracts, part-time, job sharing etc), sometimes poorly paid, and with limited social security and pension entitlements (Furlong and Cartmel, 2004; MacDonald and Marsh, 2005; MacDonald et al, 2005; MacDonald, 2011; Shildrick et al, 2012). In 2013, the last year for which there are available data, 43% of young people (aged 14–24) worked on a temporary contract, while 32% were in part-time employment (Eurostat, 2015b). This part-time working was often not voluntary but reflected a lack of better opportunities and preferred alternatives. These structural changes in employment mean that for many young people career paths have become fragmented, and many experience recurring unemployment.

High levels of youth unemployment, unstable employment and erratic career paths have therefore become key characteristics of the post-Fordist industrial and economic systems in Europe. This instability leads to precarious workers being employed in non-standard forms of employment with a high risk of recurring unemployment (Paugam, 2000; Castel, 2004; Standing, 2014; della Porta et al, 2015). Scholars have attributed the causes of this combination of high and sustained (youth) unemployment and precarity to deindustrialisation and automation processes, and the new global geography of supply chains, labour markets and post-Fordist industrial production processes, such as just-in-time or lean production models (Pugliese, 1993; Moretti, 2012). Together, deindustrialisation and automatisation have destroyed many jobs in the manufacturing sectors of developed societies, which previously employed large numbers of workers. These lost manufacturing jobs have not been fully compensated for by increased employment opportunities in either services or emerging technology. As pointed out by Kupchan, while General Motors, which is valued at $35 billion, has 77,000 employees in the US and 208,000 worldwide, Facebook, whose estimated value is $70 billion, employs approximately 2,000 workers (Kupchan, 2012: 64–5). Moreover, jobs in manufacturing industry which required fewer qualifications were among the first to be lost in the deindustrialisation process, making workers with lower educational qualifications and fewer skills less employable than before (Therborn, 1986). Moreover, in societies where employment developed along a hierarchical or pyramid structure – with adult males at the peak and young people, migrants and women at the base – those at the bottom lost out most heavily. The few jobs and the subsidies made available generally went to adult males, as officially recognised breadwinners (Pugliese, 1993).

Deindustrialisation, automation and globalisation have therefore transformed labour markets, with jobs in the manufacturing sector being outsourced to developing countries, where production costs are lower due to an abundance of cheap labour (Alpert et al, 2011). This phenomenon contributed to reducing jobs (and wages) in developed countries. In an effort to remain competitive in the global arena, many governments in the developed North promoted changes in their labour markets through deregulation. Such changes were aimed at making labour markets more 'flexible', as the economic orthodoxy was that employment regulation was detrimental to job creation. Changing industrial relations has been another tool which several states have used to attract new production and additional investment. Both collective bargaining with trade unions and general social dialogue were regarded as inappropriate for the new, just-in-time, model of industrial production believed to be required in the global economy (Baccaro and Howell, 2010; Baglioni and Brandl, 2011). However, in the majority of European countries there is little evidence that these radical reforms in European labour markets and employment policy succeeded in increasing youth employment.

Social innovation and employment

In addition to the changes mentioned earlier, policy makers at both national and supranational (EU) levels have approached the issue of youth unemployment with a combination of so-called 'passive' and 'active' policies: respectively, those focused on income support, and those focused on increasing employability. Although these vary across different countries, a common trend across all policies aimed at tackling youth (un)employment has been the active role played by civil society organisations in developing innovative solutions.

As in other policy domains, social innovations addressing unemployment are highly context-dependent and have developed diverse forms reflecting particular policy contexts and welfare regimes. Figure 5.1 summarises the different paths which social innovations in the employment sector have followed. In neo-corporatist policy systems there is a convention that state and social partners cooperate on policy, and civil society organisations (such as religious institutions) play an important policy implementation role. In this context, social innovations are generated through cooperation between a complex constellation of actors. Public and private (both commercial and not-for-profit) operators share resources and develop innovative initiatives in collaboration. This describes the various employment programmes developed in Germany, discussed below.

In contrast, to this are countries such as Sweden. Here the state has traditionally monopolised policy design and delivery, and there is a wide provision of measures to support citizens' welfare, including employment services. In this context, public actors play a central if not monopolistic role in promoting social innovation.

Finally, in contexts such as the Netherlands and United Kingdom, policy making has traditionally been characterised by the interplay of a plurality of organisations, and the state has relied largely on the market and civil society organisations to deliver policy. Private actors (often commercial enterprises) have had a leading role in developing social innovation responses to employment, which cooperate with or are procured by public agencies. The examples discussed in the following section illustrate these variations.

Figure 5.1: Social innovation and employment in different policy contexts

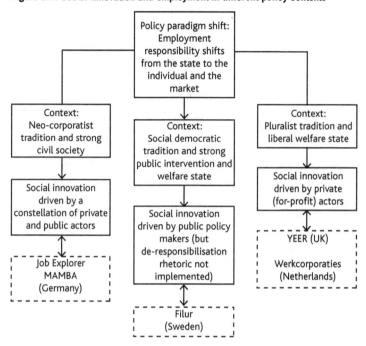

Social innovation in corporatist, pluralist and state-centred policy contexts

Employers are often reluctant to hire young people immediately after they have completed their education. Many employers regard inexperienced younger recruits as posing greater risk, such as failing to satisfy customers' or users' demands, production mistakes or general unreliability. For their part, younger people often have unrealistic expectations about employment and preferences that do not correspond with real working experience or opportunities. Reflecting these perceptual barriers, much of the attention in youth employment policy has been on easing the transition from school to employment. This has led to various initiatives, such as internships and apprenticeships, as well as programmes offering students opportunities to spend a portion of their education on a placement where they acquire practical employment experience. Several social innovations have sought to foster mutual understanding and trust between employers and young people. Such initiatives also build bridges and improve communication between unconnected actors, which is a key feature of social innovation. The optimal time for such activity is the stage at which they start thinking about what kind of job they would like and what opportunities are available locally. Providing accurate information about work and relevant employment experience is crucial to prevent young people from developing unrealistic expectations about the requirements and terms and conditions of employment, and therefore avoiding a potential spiral of disillusionment, demotivation and unemployment. Similarly, it can be beneficial for employers to counteract any ignorance and prejudice they may have so that they are more open to potential younger recruits. Several social innovations operate to create these mutually beneficial conditions and outcomes. Those discussed below address two key concerns of contemporary youth employment policy: how to persuade employers to hire younger workers, and how to persuade younger people of the attractiveness of particular jobs or sectors.

Germany illustrates the role and impact of social innovations in a corporatist public policy configuration and occupational welfare state. It also provides an example of how policy responsibility has shifted from the state to the individual job seekers and the market. One example of an employment social innovation in this context is the Job Explorer programme in the Friedrichshain-Kreuzberg district of Berlin (Ewert and Evers, 2014). This has several innovative features: it focuses on a particular category of young people at an important age; it provides a range of support services; it involves cooperation between a range of public and private actors; and it engages with young people and employers to challenge their mutual prejudices and potential misunderstandings. Each of these aspects merits further consideration.

The age focus is an important feature of the Job Explorer programme: it is aimed at secondary school pupils aged between 13 and 17. This is a critical juncture – when young people are starting to develop ideas about what they would like to do after they leave school, and when positive employment experiences may be decisive in preventing problems and enabling young people to embark on a positive working life. The programme provides early experience of vocational training, jobs and the labour market in general, starting three years before these students complete their high school education.

The Job Explorer team works with schools to gather information about what kind of job or career each young person would like or can imagine undertaking. This is followed by a 'reality check', where pupils are offered the possibility of experiencing such a job by visiting relevant employers for a couple of hours after school each week. The aim of this second step is to make young people more aware of what this job entails and how it may differ from their expectations, while also sensitising employers to the young people's skills and talent (Ewert and Evers, 2014).

As is characteristic of a social innovation in a neo-corporatist welfare environment, Job Explorer – a publicly funded initiative – relies on the capacity to build effective partnerships among a range of actors. These include both public organisations (schools, local municipalities and the Job Explorer team) and private sector bodies (local employers' associations). The Job Explorer team invests considerable time and social capital to connect with potential employers, through local business associations, to persuade them that engaging with the programme enables them to scout prospective employees and future talent more effectively. The case is also made that participation in the programme contributes to community wellbeing, thereby fulfilling both corporate and social objectives (Ewert and Evers, 2014).

A similar pattern of multi-societal partnership (and policy responsibility shift) is evident in another German employment social innovation. This initiative aims to increase employment opportunities for immigrants who, like younger people, often struggle to enter the labour market. Immigrants and refugees face several barriers to labour market integration. These include the attitudes and stereotypes of some employers; bureaucratic hurdles; and particular characteristics which disadvantage some potential employees, such as language proficiency, insufficient relevant skills or a lack of recognised qualifications. In such cases social innovations need to both enhance the capabilities of their clients and address the social and institutional impediments they encounter.

Developed by a local branch of the Gemeinnützige Gesellschaft zur Unterstützung Asylsuchender e.V. (GGUA) – the association for relief of refugees (a civil society organisation working with refugees) – the MAMBA programme trains and mentors immigrants and refugees seeking employment, and collaborates with employers to increase employment opportunities for this marginalised group (Boadu et al, 2014). The MAMBA programme offers services to improve the skills and qualifications of immigrants and refugees, such as language and computer courses. It also provides assistance to deal with administrative procedures, such as obtaining residence and work permits. MAMBA staff also work with employers' associations to counteract prejudice against hiring migrants and refugees.

The innovative character of the MAMBA programme stems from its capacity to connect multiple private and public sector partners in a network which exchanges human, intellectual, relational and material resources to meet the employment target (Boadu et al, 2014). In many countries a job is a condition of legal residence for immigrants and refugees. This initiative seeks to empower beneficiaries by highlighting and enhancing their skills, knowledge and employment potential. This is intended to help prevent longer-term social exclusion and related problems, and to enhance social cohesion. The administrative support MAMBA provides to clients eases the work of some public officials and may therefore save public resources.

Social innovations addressing employment challenges take a different form in countries where social welfare provision has traditionally been dominated by public sector actors. The Filur project in the Swedish capital, Stockholm, provides an example of this.

Like Job Explorer in Berlin, Filur aims to facilitate young people's entry into the labour market by providing them with practical work experiences and offering opportunities for potential employees and employers to interact (Nordfeldt and Carrigan, 2014). Filur resembles the Job Explorer programme in being structured across several steps.

First, participants (aged 16–25) complete eight weeks of needs assessment and pedagogic-psychological motivation training. This is followed by four weeks' employment experience in a sector or company in which they are interested. Participants also receive two hours of mentoring per month from someone working in their chosen occupation or sector.

However, unlike the Job Explorer programme, but consistent with the Swedish model of welfare and social policy, the Filur project is run entirely by public sector actors. Filur is administered by the municipal office in charge of job placement, it is funded by public money (the European Social Fund), and the managing board includes only public sector representatives (Nordfeldt and Carrigan, 2014). The official justification for having only civil servants on the managing team is efficiency. However, such public sector dominance is typical of social innovations in a context where the state continues to plays a central role in social policy, despite the recent implementation of some neoliberal welfare adaptations and policies (Persson and Hafen, 2014).

A third form of social innovation in employment is provided by countries with a tradition of pluralist policy making and where civil society actors have played a leading role in promoting and implementing policy. This describes the situation in England – as it is increasingly questionable whether there exists a shared UK or British welfare system or social innovation culture (Mooney and Scott, 2016). One example of this is the Youth, Employment and Enterprise Rehearsal (YEER) initiative in Birmingham (Brookes et al, 2014). In 2010 a community interest company, the Future Melting Pot, launched a pilot project aimed at raising employment opportunities for minority ethnic young people who were not in employment, education or training (so-called 'NEETs'). The project was intended to support participants to set up their own business.

> YEER was designed to provide business specific training and assist young people from developing an idea to starting their own business. The project included training, support and access to accredited advisors. The approach could be characterised as

intensive, personalised support to stimulate entrepreneurialism. (Brookes et al, 2014: 387)

In this respect, it is a classic example of policy responsibility shift and welfare marketisation – where unemployed people are urged to create *their own* job opportunities. Nevertheless, as the purpose of YEER is to empower and help young people at risk of long-term social and economic exclusion, it could be regarded as a social innovation. Furthermore, the project employs innovative social media tools to help reach young people (Brookes et al, 2014).

Another employment social innovation developed in the context of a strong private sector policy presence is the werkcorporaties (work corporations) developed in the Dutch city of Nijmegen. As Broersma et al point out, this initiative is emblematic of the shift in responsibility for employment from public to private actors:

The need for rearranging re-employment services was given by the financial cutbacks that were imposed by national government. In fact, the municipal budget of 26 million Euro for re-employment in 2012 would be brought down to 13 million Euro in 2013 and eventually to 8 million Euro in 2014 and thereafter. Hence, in order to 'realize the ambitions' of the municipality with respect to re-employment, the municipality was forced to adapt their current policy in an 'innovative fashion'. This meant the reduction of subsidised jobs to zero, the creation of work corporations and cooperation between municipal organisations that were dependent on subsidised employees. (Broersma et al, 2014: 226)

These work corporations are programmes contracted out by municipalities to private (not-for-profit) organisations to equip younger people who have been made redundant with the skills, knowledge and relational capital required to find a new job. Service users are given the opportunity to receive training and work experience and regular employment-related education. Current work corporations involved in the programme operate in a range of sectors and industries, such as construction and green maintenance, fashion, catering and running a solar-powered tourist bus. Although participants are not paid, they do receive social protection benefits. The service is designed to provide short-term support for a maximum of two years.

Case Study: Zero Chômage

Zero Chômage is a social innovation in France, initiated by a civil society organisation with strategic support from public actors and public funding. It builds on three core principles. First, the belief that no one is really 'unemployable' – people possess and retain their competencies and skill when unemployed. Second, that communities have unmet needs and consideration should therefore be given to how these can be addressed by involving people whose skills are unused due to unemployment. Third, long-term unemployment results in costs for communities which have to pay social welfare benefits and also lose the services and contributions which could be provided by those outside the labour market.

The Zero Chômage initiative is based on the idea that the resources committed to support the long-term unemployed should be utilised more productively. It proposes that these resources should be used to create local companies which hire long-term unemployed people on open-ended contracts, to perform jobs which the unemployed people have themselves devised, based on their own interests and capacities, and which address an unmet community need. By this means, the community would become a 'zero-unemployed' area (Zero Chômage), as all long-term unemployed workers could be hired to perform socially useful work.

In France the idea was originally promoted by a civil society organisation called France Quart Monde. It has advocated creating social enterprises, called Entreprises à but d'emploi (EBE), which offer eligible unemployed people an open-ended contract to develop or take up a job which addresses the needs of either the local community or a local private sector company, on condition that this job does not compete with any existing ones. This condition is monitored by a governance system involving trade unions, local authorities and employers' representatives.

Zero Chômage contrasts with most existing active labour market and employment services, because it generates new jobs based on the skills and interests of unemployed people themselves. Funding for any newly created companies and jobs comes from the public money that would otherwise support the income of the unemployed and from local development projects. Zero Chômage is an example of the 'complementary economy' – a hybrid form of enterprise which combines private sector management processes with public funding and a business model which does not compete with conventional companies.

National policy makers have been persuaded to launch a nationwide experiment to implement EBEs in 10 communities with populations between 5,000 and 10,000 people. The programme was launched in November 2016 and is planned to run for five years. It involves 100–200 people in each community, and will create an estimated 2,000 new jobs. Some examples of jobs created in rural areas of the programme include roles supporting the delivery of community transport services for older people and those with mobility impairments, safe transport for children and home-delivered library services.

Comparing and contrasting employment social innovations

These various social innovations supporting employment demonstrate both similarities and differences. The differences reflect their respective policy and institutional settings. The similarities arise as they express the same overall shift in policy responsibility: from the state and public actors to individuals, private and civil society organisations, and the market.

Social innovations are context-dependent and need to be understood in relation to their particular institutional and cultural conditions (Sinclair and Baglioni, 2014). Understanding the role and operation of social innovations addressing employment issues requires consideration of their general institutional context and the policy-making regimes and particular welfare traditions which condition them. The first policy regime considered above is corporatism – where the state works in partnership with formally recognised social actors, whose participation in policy making is institutionalised. An alternative is pluralism – where the state operates as a broker mediating between multiple social actors, and where private sector companies are pivotal in policy design and delivery. These alternative policy regimes are related to different welfare traditions. In social democratic systems the state plays a dominant role, affording only an ancillary position to civil society actors. In conservative or continental regimes, welfare is delivered by state and private actors in partnership, and private actors are often faith-based organisations. Finally, in liberal welfare states a leading role in service provision is taken by private sector and civil society organisations.

The examples of social innovation which we have discussed exemplify these different forms of policy development and delivery. For example, in the corporatist German system the social innovations involved in employment have been created through the joint effort of public and private actors. In the social democratic system, represented by Sweden, the social innovation was state-initiated and left little space for other actors to emerge. In this context the state has only conceded a significant or leading role to social actors where it accepts that they are better able to reach particular beneficiaries (for example, immigrants) and integrate them into the community. Finally, in more liberal welfare regimes, such as the Netherlands and parts of the UK, employment social innovations have been developed and led by civil society or private sector organisations. These have often emerged in response to the reduction or withdrawal of public funds, and have then been used by the public sector as templates for further policy innovation.

Despite such differences, these social innovations demonstrate similar underlying political philosophies and shared operational principles. They all regard unemployment (and in particular the unemployment of vulnerable groups, such as young people, immigrants or women) as a failure of individual capacity to enter or remain in the labour market. Reflecting this diagnosis, these initiatives prescribe increasing service users' 'employability'. This ambitious and complex goal is to be achieved by introducing participants as early as possible to the labour market, and equipping them with the knowledge and skills considered essential to find employment. In many cases, the ultimate proposal to solve the supposed employment deficiencies of those at the bottom of the recruitment pool is for these people to create their own jobs: to become (self-)entrepreneurs or, in some cases, social entrepreneurs.

In this respect, many examples of social innovation in employment are a measure of last resort, introduced only when other options have failed. This raises the question of whether these initiatives ought to be regarded as genuine social innovations which empower people and improve lives, prevent social problems, and enhance overall public welfare.

Case study: LAMH Recycle

LAMH Recycle is a small social innovation developed in response to the need to create new businesses and generate employment opportunities in a relatively deprived Scottish community marked by high unemployment. It aims to increase the labour market opportunities of those who have experienced long-term unemployed due to health issues, personal circumstances or a lack of experience.

LAMH recycle is a social enterprise providing training and employment to unemployed people in the growing market of IT and electrical product waste management and recycling. It has a particular focus on repairing, recycling and selling PCs which would otherwise be discarded. This social business offers training, support and real work experience to long-term unemployed people; in particular, it strengthens their soft skills, such as time-keeping and regular attendance, communication, self-esteem and motivation. It also addresses a growing issue of resource depletion and environmental hazard.

LAMH recycle has become a business partner of local authorities and several private companies. It also provides a community service by selling repaired IT equipment at low cost to those who might not otherwise be able to purchase such products.

Conclusion

As with some of the social innovations considered in previous chapters, the direct beneficiaries of the employment social innovations discussed above are not 'ordinary' citizens and mainstream service users. In fact, these social innovations are targeted to help particular vulnerable or marginalised groups: refugees and immigrants, younger people, or those whose social citizenship entitlements are reduced or exhausted by long-term unemployment. The less exceptional needs of ordinary citizens are addressed by more conventional welfare services. This suggests that the question of whether such social innovations provide citizenship-based guaranteed entitlements equivalent to mainstream public welfare services may be misguided, or is at least partial. In many cases these social innovations are niche services catering for additional or exceptional needs. Their improvised and semi-institutionalised character reflects this role and the distinctive challenges which it presents. Indeed, the effect of some of these social innovations is to broaden the scope of social citizenship and extend it to non-nationals.

These social innovations are designed to prevent social and economic exclusion, as they address needs related to (un)employment. However, it is questionable whether they could be regarded as moving upstream and preventing problems, as most of them are local, small-scale projects, while unemployment, and in particular youth unemployment, is a problem affecting millions. To be effectively preventative, such measures require a strong connection with wider social and economic development policies and the conditions which they address. Some of these innovations enhance participants' employment skills through providing training in such areas as language, IT, and business and trading regulation. In addition, however, the training, mentoring and networking opportunities that they also provide may improve participants' overall capacity and social capital. On the other hand, some of these social innovations amount to gambles on the capacity of vulnerable groups (for example, young people, immigrants) to develop their own businesses, when creating and sustaining *any* enterprise is a demanding task, and is particularly risky in a challenging economic environment. Therefore, even if these innovations do prevent some problems, they may generate others for those they are intended to help and the welfare services to which they may need to turn.

The relationship between these social innovations and existing institutions and public welfare providers varies with the welfare regime and policy context. In some cases, social innovations and public agencies cooperate fully and effectively, to the point where it is difficult to distinguish one from the other. In other settings, social innovations have been intentionally created to fill a gap vacated by public spending cuts or state withdrawal. It is therefore difficult to generalise about the nature and effect of social innovations in this respect.

Overall, several social innovations in the employment sector have introduced changes and achieved improvement through offering empowerment opportunities otherwise unavailable to particularly disadvantaged groups. However, the scale of the unemployment problem is too large to be addressed effectively by even the most innovative ad hoc, local, sometimes episodic and small-scale solutions. Most of the examples of social innovation considered here do not contest the neoliberal economic philosophy which has reshaped employment policy in the twenty-first century. Rather, they have been conceived within and conditioned by this approach. However, these examples also demonstrate that there may be enough passion within communities and among social innovators to enable an alternative perspective, which challenges the dominance of the neoliberal approach, to emerge over time.

Note

[1] http://ec.europa.eu/eurostat/statistics-explained/index.php/Unemployment_statistics

SIX

Conclusion

Social innovations include many imaginative and inspirational initiatives from across the world which address complex and deeply troubling social problems. Whether they are providing care and accommodation to those who are homeless; helping to rebuild the lives of people recovering from addiction; bringing education, culture and beauty to neglected neighbourhoods and benighted communities; or offering fellowship and new opportunities to learn, work and contribute to marginalised and truly disadvantaged groups, the considerable good that social innovations have done deserves recognition. Social innovations combine the energy and optimism of their founders and stakeholders with new ways of responding to social problems. They have harnessed the power of social capital, the dynamism of enterprise and, in many cases, the opportunities created by new technologies, to provide help and hope to groups which have been overlooked or excluded by mainstream society. Social innovations also often emerge at the frontiers between different sectors, to create hybrid organisations and forge new collaborative relationships between service users and disparate stakeholders. In doing so they bring together dispersed assets and improvise imaginative coordinated responses to wicked social problems. Any evaluation or critique of social innovations must be tempered with admiration for what that they have accomplished, often with very limited resources in some of the most demanding conditions and circumstances which have defeated and caused despair in others.

Nevertheless, it is the responsibility of policy analysts to independently scrutinise and appraise social interventions, and social innovations are no exception. Although they may be mainly autonomous third sector organisations, many social innovations either already receive some form of public subsidy or investment, or some of their staunchest supporters argue that their role in social and public policy should be extended. It is therefore not only legitimate but essential that the principles, operation and impact of social innovations are examined carefully. Social innovations may have many virtues, but they entail opportunity costs – and potentially risks – which must be considered; not least because 'The social innovation concept has been put forward to pursue extremely ambitious objectives. However, there is at the time of writing only limited proof of whether social innovation can or already has delivered on some of its promises' (Grimm et al, 2013: 451).

Our aims in this book have been twofold. First, to advance understanding of this relatively unfamiliar concept among social and public policy analysts; and second, to outline the questions which such analysts ask of social innovation. Chapters 1 and 2 clarified what social innovation is, considered why it is currently fashionable, and showed how it relates to more familiar concepts and debates in social and public policy analysis. Chapters 3–5 provided examples illustrating how social innovations have operated in relation to food security, social care and employment, and considered their impact in these areas. We hope that this discussion and analysis will help readers to judge how significant social innovation is or might be in addressing social problems and promoting welfare.

In this concluding chapter we highlight some of the main themes which emerge from our evidence and commentary, and what we conclude these suggest about the capacity of social innovation to deliver significant social improvements. We then offer some final reflections on what a truly radical and transformational form of social innovation could look like and what it could accomplish in social and public policy.

Case Study: Homeless World Cup

The Homeless World Cup uses the global popularity of football to help homeless people change their lives and to challenge perceptions of the causes and victims of homelessness. It was established in 2001 as a social enterprise and charity, and now operates in 70 countries through designated national partners, which promote grassroots football development programmes designed to help homeless people. Its most high-profile activity is an annual international football tournament, held in a different country each year, involving homeless participants from across the world. The 2016 event was held in Glasgow and involved over 500 male and female participants from 52 different countries; over 80,000 spectators watched the tournament. The 2017 Homeless World Cup was held in Oslo.

Supporters of the Homeless World Cup argue that participants improve both their physical fitness and mental wellbeing through the discipline of regular training sessions and by participating in a team sport. They also claim that competing and cooperating with others to represent their country in a prestigious event has a marked impact on participants' self-esteem and confidence. Research suggests that Homeless World Cup participants are more likely to undertake or remain in substance misuse rehabilitation programmes, and that the experience itself alleviates some of the symptoms and damaging effects of mental illness. Participants also have improved access to medical and social support systems, and report increased motivation and capacity to reintegrate into mainstream society (Sherry and O'May, 2013).

A further benefit claimed for the Homeless World Cup is that it raises public awareness of homelessness and increases support for people who are homeless. Participants are able to demonstrate their skills and dedication to an international audience, thereby challenging some of the negative perceptions of homeless people. A survey of spectators at the Glasgow 2016 event found that 83% had a more positive opinion of people experiencing homelessness as a result of attending the tournament (Thomson, 2017).

The operation and impact of social innovation

Chapters 1 and 2 set out a number of questions which social innovation raises for social and public policy analysis, as well as the kinds of questions which such analysis poses for social innovation. The evidence and examples presented in Chapters 3, 4 and 5 allow some comments to be made in response to these questions. First, there is the issue of whether social innovations could be described as providing better services than conventional public welfare; that is, are they more cost-effective, responsive or superior in some other important regard? The first point to note in relation to this is that social innovations are simply too diverse in function, scale and context to enable any meaningful generalisations about their impact or cost-effectiveness relative to alternatives. There is also still insufficient robust comparative evidence to make definitive general statements about the ratio of the costs of social innovations to their outcomes. However, it does seem clear that social innovations are not necessarily a cheaper or easier option than mainstream services. This should not be surprising, as they often involve complex inter-sectoral partnerships, combining several different functions addressing multiple complex issues. Indeed, it can be challenging to monitor and evaluate the activities, resources used or outputs produced by some social innovations, as many develop and operate through improvisation. This can be unnerving for some public officials and elected policy makers, who may be reluctant to support experiments with imprecise outcomes or where the risk of failure is difficult to predict. The ambiguity of their inputs and outcomes also makes it difficult to establish a business case for some social innovations. This is one reason why relatively few social innovations are commercially viable propositions and many rely upon various forms of public subsidy, including indirect support (such as concessions, rebates and favourable operating conditions). Such support might be considered reasonable, given that social innovations aim to address neglected social issues and unrewarding conditions, and it is unrealistic to expect them to turn a profit from such activities.

Empowering and enhancing the capabilities of service users appear to be strengths of social innovations. But this is also tautological, as these features are integral to the definition of social innovation and involved in selecting the evidence and cases typically used to illustrate it. Nevertheless, social innovations reinforce what is already known about the benefits to service users of co-production: unsurprisingly, enabling and respectful services generally achieve better outcomes than provision delivered without care or concern for users' agency. Participatory interventions which enhance capabilities are more effective than treating people as passive recipients. More interesting than the efficacy of participatory provision per se is what lessons social innovation experiments provide about how to facilitate co-production. One important but potentially discouraging lesson is that developing and delivering empowering personalised services is not cheap in the short term. However, there are potential longer-term savings and individual and social benefits to be gained by investing in the kinds of intensive tailored social support which many social innovations provide.

There is no clear or consistent evidence that social innovations are significantly better than conventional social protection systems in 'moving upstream' and applying a preventative approach to social problems. There are few social innovations which could be said to have fundamentally reshaped the circumstances and conditions which created the problems they address. The causes of these conditions are both deeper and larger than social innovations alone can change. Social innovations (valuable, responsive and respectful to service users though they may be) generally ameliorate egregious social conditions; very few have the capacity to remove or fundamentally reform their structural causes. In this respect, social innovations are comparable to cooperatives in the nineteenth century: they offer alternatives to mainstream services and systems but adapt to rather than themselves revolutionise the socioeconomic and political landscape. The cooperative movement only became a potent transformational force when it became allied to or helped establish political strategies and associations. There is as yet no social innovation equivalent of a labour movement or social democratic parties; therefore, its political influence remains indirect and partial. Nevertheless, some social innovations do influence policy in two important respects. First, social innovations may provide examples of alternative approaches, models and delivery options which can attract the attention of policy makers and encourage mimicry and policy learning. A second related influence is that such innovative approaches demonstrate new possibilities and operating models. In this way social innovations can reframe how social issues are conceived and – under favourable political conditions – may encourage policy makers and other stakeholders to rethink some of their assumptions about the causes of and most effective responses to troubling social conditions.

The relationship between social innovations and public welfare institutions (such as local government) is variable and complex. In some cases this relationship is not only harmonious but co-dependent; in other cases social innovations grate against and conflict with existing welfare institutions. Chapter 5 provided examples of social innovations in the area of employment and active labour market policy which were developed in partnership with and in some cases led by government. In contrast, in the area of food poverty (Chapter 3), there is much less of a tradition of government activity; here social innovations and civil society organisations are considerably more proactive and have intervened to fill what is an increasingly evident and concerning gap in provision. The care sector (Chapter 4) has examples of both considerable public sector activity and significant omissions and under-provision. This is also an area where the intrepreneurial imagination and advocacy of public officials and service professionals has been particularly important. In this respect, the social innovation literature provides a useful corrective to commentators who equate entrepreneurship with the private sector.

Across all of these fields the evidence suggests that social innovations are rarely entirely independent of the public sector. As they often rely upon governments for support (or for permission and licences to operate), they accommodate to rather than conflict with or transform the public welfare environment. The role that social innovations play in welfare seems largely conditioned by existing institutions and policy decisions: they generally mould themselves to fit the spaces available to them in the institutional landscape, and do either what they are allowed to or what no one else will. In this respect, although social innovations might shape the boundaries of the welfare landscape, they do not radically transform it. However, it is perhaps misleading to think of social innovations developing 'outside' of or in opposition to existing welfare systems; instead, they should be regarded as developing in symbiosis with existing institutions and infrastructures.

It is also important to remember that the role and position of social innovations in relation to both the state and private sectors are not fixed but dynamic. As was shown in the case of employability policy, a degree of state withdrawal or 'privatisation' opens up greater scope for social innovation activity. Whether this is a welcome development, leads to better outcomes or is within the capacity of social innovations to deliver are partly matters of judgement, and also questions which require further analysis.

Some social welfare services are indispensable both for society in general and for those who depend upon them. They are mechanisms for guaranteeing fundamental human rights and meeting essential needs. Such services must therefore be reliable and delivered equally to all eligible recipients across diverse settings and conditions within national frameworks. These requirements relate to the transferability, sustainability and scaling up of social innovations. Regarding transferability first of all, the evidence suggests that the most effective social innovations are rooted in the experiences, conditions and preferences of their communities and users. Social innovations are often the products of particular environments and develop in response to specific conditions and challenges. Relatively few social innovations can have been successfully directly copied and duplicated across diverse cultural frontiers and institutional environments. The example of the *condominio solidale* in Bologna – which put together older native residents with immigrant families (Chapter 4) – suggests that, unless they are compatible with the host body, then transplanted social innovations are rejected or produce unexpected side effects. However, even if social innovations cannot be directly replicated, the best of them still offer lessons and models which can be borrowed from and adapted to new conditions. This implies that perhaps what ought to be transferred is not so much the specific practice of social innovation as the imagination and drive to improve services which characterises the best of these endeavours.

In relation to their scale of operation, there are relatively few examples of sustained and successful societal-wide (let alone international) social innovations. As noted above, some social innovations may have a national level impact by 'educating' policy makers and stakeholders, for example, providing alternative models which are adapted and adopted by others. They may also become absorbed within national welfare systems and policies, and thus reform these internally rather than develop visibly distinct structures. Some social innovations might therefore be scaled up by infecting the internal nervous systems of national welfare systems, rather than by creating entirely separate bodies. To have a more visible external transformational impact, social innovations would need to take on the campaigning and political activities of social movements. Very few have the interest or capacity to do this.

Finally, there is the question of whether social innovations provide services with the same citizenship entitlements that many conventional public welfare services guarantee. This is a potential criticism of social innovations: often they cannot provide the same rights or security of provision offered by conventional state-backed welfare. On the other hand, many social innovations extend the scope of welfare provision – covering unmet needs and/or underserved groups, such as migrants, minority ethnic communities and disabled people. By highlighting and (partially) meeting such needs, social innovations may increase awareness of unmet demand and encourage the expansion and coverage of social protection, so that new rights are institutionalised. Interest in the role of social innovations is also growing at a time when various existing welfare rights are being eroded in many societies. Many welfare entitlements are less secure than before, so that the distinction in this regard between state and social innovation social services is now less clear cut. Indeed, social innovations may be promoted by some as an alternative to or substitute for public citizenship rights and – as mentioned in Chapter 2 – could become implicated in this ideological withdrawal of the state.

Most social innovations develop in the service sector. This is not only because much of social welfare provision involves delivering services in one form or another, but also because service innovation is relatively quick and inexpensive, involving less upfront capital investment than the research and development usually required for new products or technology in other economic sectors (Evers et al, 2014: 17). These issues of resources and limited scale and capacity are central to any analysis of social innovation. Even staunch advocates recognise that few social innovations have had truly transformational effects: 'even the impact of bodies such as AA or OhmyNews are not in the same scale as the impact of truly systemic innovations like parliamentary democracy, the Internet, integrated childcare or zero carbon cities' (Mulgan et al, 2007a: 23). Social innovations may have improved the distribution of food, the delivery of social care or the responsiveness of employment training programmes, but they have not reduced food poverty, social isolation and neglect, or unemployment per se.

It is telling that there is as yet no example of a social innovation which has demonstrated the ability to provide public goods or deliver mainstream services of general interest on a macro-social scale for a sustained period. The possibility of a social innovation providing a core and mass welfare service – such as social security benefits or pensions – currently seems remote. Therefore, as things stand it seems that social innovation can only be a supplement to more established and reliable forms and systems of welfare provision. Some can serve specific needs and be effective in a 'very marginal niche for a period', but they complement core welfare institutions which remain the principal components of social and public policy (Mulgan et al, 2007a: 23)

This is less a criticism of social innovation than a dose of healthy realism. After all, it is a rather tall order to expect what are often small, localised initiatives to meet challenging social conditions or chronic support needs; to pioneer experimental business models, with no or minimal subsidy, which cost less than but outperform public services; and to do all this in a participatory and empowering way, and to ultimately transform the conditions which gave rise to these initiatives in the first place. If social innovations are delivering social value then shouldn't they receive public sector support or subsidy? And if a viable income could be made from addressing problematic conditions and meeting social needs then wouldn't the private sector already be serving them? When social innovations have found ways to combine social benefit with financial sustainability (for example, by developing mutual financial services and credit organisations in Europe in the nineteenth century) private enterprises have moved in to exploit this market opportunity (Mulgan, et al, 2007a: 14–15).

Case study: Grameen Bank

The Grameen Bank has become one of the most renowned and lauded social innovations in the world, garnering its founder Professor Muhammad Yunus many accolades, including the 2006 Nobel Peace Prize. Alongside the Bangladesh Rural Advancement Committee (BRAC), Grameen is regarded as a pioneer of microfinance. The bank originated in 1976 when Muhammad Yunus started providing small loans at low interest rates to very low-income borrowers in Jobra, a rural area of Bangladesh (*grameen* is the Bengali word for 'rural' or 'village').

Microfinance (often known as microcredit or microlending) fills a need for affordable credit not previously adequately met by either conventional banks or governments. Low-income households need access to credit to manage their budgets and invest in any opportunities for enterprise or development that may arise. However, without collateral against which borrowing can be secured, they either have nowhere to turn, or rely upon unregulated lenders (including loan sharks) who may charge very high or even extortionate interest rates. The Grameen Bank developed a model of group lending which enabled low-income borrowers to pool resources and collectively commit to repay members' loans. As a result, Grameen was able to reduce both default rates and the costs of providing credit to high-risk, low-income borrowers.

Grameen received initial support from a nationalised bank in Bangladesh and several international donors. It became a formal independent bank in 1983 and a corporate bank in 2002. Today, 90% of its shares are owned by its borrowers while 10% are held by the Bangladeshi government. It is estimated that the Grameen Bank in Bangladesh has nearly nine million borrowers, 95% of whom are women. Globally, an estimated 75% of microcredit borrowers are women (New Internationalist, nd). The success of the Grameen Bank has led to a range of social businesses, the Grameen Creative Lab and partnerships with global companies, such as Adidas. One such venture is Grameen Danone Foods Ltd, which produces low-cost, fortified nutritional yoghurt aimed at children in low-income households.

Microcredit has been hailed as a financial and social innovation that has transformed millions of lives in the developing world, and numerous variants of the Grameen model have been established in Latin America, Africa and Asia. However, evidence of the effectiveness of microcredit in reducing poverty is complex and contested. One critic estimates that only 5% of Grameen borrowers escape poverty for a sustained period as a direct result of microcredit (Roodman, 2012).

Some microfinance institutions have been accused of profiteering and burdening very poor households with unrepayable debts. The typical interest rate for a Grameen loan is about 20%, and the international average is 37%. However, other microcredit lenders charge interest rates of 70% or more (New Internationalist, nd). This is attributed to commercial providers who have sought to profit from the growing demand for microfinance, and abandoned the social principles of pioneers such as Grameen.

Microfinance provides an essential service in a new and potentially empowering way, and the Grameen Bank has inspired many new social business models. Whether it is appropriate to or viable in developed countries which have established social welfare systems remains to be seen. Overall, its impact – significant though it is – may be conditional and limited.

Some commentators and policy makers have perhaps pinned too much hope on social innovations and been encouraged by their inspirational dynamism to exaggerate their impact and potential significance. Social innovations may be an example of what the marketing company Gartner (n.d.) call the 'Hype Cycle'. This describes the reactions some technological innovations generate. The first stage in this process is the trigger that inspires the innovation which then receives enthusiastic support. This leads to stage two, where there is a 'peak of inflated expectations'. Stage three is reached when these expectations are not met and there is a 'trough of disillusionment'. However, some innovations progress to stage four, the 'slope of enlightenment', where the genuine possibilities of the innovation are realised. Finally, in stage five, there is a 'plateau of productivity', where the innovation is applied in an effective and useful way. In some circles, social innovation is at stage two. However, stage four is more realistic and productive for social and public policy analysis and practice; and perhaps, with a more tempered and evidence-based approach to social innovation, the disappointment and setbacks of stage three can be circumvented.

Working against this possibility is the fact that social innovations are an example of what Smith calls a 'chameleonic' concept in social and public policy (2013: 192). Such ideas can be interpreted in many different ways and endorsed by a variety of advocates. They often have highly vocal champions, such as think tanks, policy advisers, academics and associations which campaign on their behalf (for example, NESTA in the UK or the Center for Social Innovation at Stanford in the US). The ambiguity of a chameleonic concept is one reason for their appeal but also a source of practical limitations. Fortunately, by necessity, social innovators and entrepreneurs are themselves usually practically minded and pragmatic, as social problems are not eased or solved by intriguing ideas and good intentions alone. Their good work continues while the debate goes on around them. But this work is not well served by hype or unrealistic expectations.

Case study: Teach for America/Teach First

Teach for America (TFA) developed from a thesis by Wendy Kopp, a student at Princeton University in 1989. Kopp proposed recruiting a cadre of high-performing graduates from the top colleges and universities in the US to teach at disadvantaged and underperforming schools. The project was in part inspired by the Peace Corp programme in the US and similar models such as Voluntary Service Overseas in the UK (Teach First, nd)

TFA applicants receive five weeks of intensive teacher training and commit to working in a school in a disadvantaged area for at least two years. TFA initially launched with 489 graduate recruits and quickly expanded, gaining substantial public and private sector support. The federal Department of Education allocated $50 million to the programme in 2010–11; a similar amount was donated by the Walton Family Foundation and a further $100 million was contributed by a consortium of private foundations and corporate donors (Ravitch, 2012). TFA is a prominent example of 'Philanthrocapitalism': where private foundations and corporate donors use contributions to social causes to advance particular ideological perspectives and political objectives (Bishop and Green, 2008).

In 2007 Kopp cofounded Teach For All to export the TFA model to other countries. A British version, called Teach First, was launched in 2002 by a member of staff at McKinsey consulting, with support from various third sector organisations, corporate social responsibility charities and the UK government. Teach First attracted 1,300 applications for 200 places in its first wave of recruitment, and applications have continued to expand each year. It initially operated in London before extending in 2006 to other parts of England and Wales. Versions of TFA have also been launched in Norway, Estonia and New Zealand.

TFA and its international variants are based partly on the belief that a key factor in unequal educational outcomes is poor-quality teaching, and that new forms of educational leadership are required to improve problem schools. Unsurprisingly, this criticism of existing provision is controversial. TFA is a highly politicised social innovation which encroaches upon established institutions and professional interests.

Evidence of the impact of TFA is equally controversial and open to interpretation. Critics of the Teach First programme in England and Wales argue that it is more generously funded than comparable mainstream provision, which compromises cost-effectiveness comparisons. TFA claims that its recruits (which it calls 'corps members') outperform existing teachers and raise educational standards and attainment among children from deprived communities. Its critics argue that being taught by inexperienced graduates is neither in the best interests of particularly vulnerable children nor a long-term solution to educational inequalities. They argue that new and unqualified graduates would not be permitted to teach in more advantaged schools, where parents would insist that their children are taught by fully trained professionals. Critics further allege that TFA attracts applicants who may only have a short-term interest in rather than a commitment to education and regard teaching as 'an experience rather than a career' (Strauss, 2011). TFA rebuts this and reports that a significant proportion of corps members remain in education beyond their initial two years.

Central to the controversy surrounding TFA is the allegation that it is motivated by a hostility towards public sector education and state welfare provision. Whether or not this is true, and whatever the merits of TFA and related initiatives, it demonstrates that social innovations are not mere technical or politically neutral responses to social problems.

Social innovation and the future of social and public policy

For all their limitations and the challenges they face, welfare institutions and systems are embedded in many societies and cannot be replaced seamlessly by social innovations without provoking potential resistance from existing providers and service users. Even if skilful political manoeuvring could initiate such a reform, few social innovations offer readymade alternatives: 'one of the central messages of our reading of the case studies on local social innovations is that they are the opposite of quick-fix-solutions' (Evers et al, 2014: 4). Nevertheless, one argument advanced by social innovation advocates does look compelling: the challenges which confront current and conventional forms of welfare provision cannot be ignored, and simply doing more of the same does not seem to be a viable option. Welfare systems need long-term, imaginative and large-scale responses to address chronic social problems and emerging demands.

Several structural factors condition and reshape public welfare systems:

- socioeconomic conditions and dynamics, such as the transition to industrial or to post-industrial systems;
- economic development and the level and distribution of resources;
- interests of collective social movements (for example, classes and parties) and the solidarity or coalitions which can be forged between them (Baldwin, 1990).

The question is whether any of these structural conditions have changed such that new welfare paradigms are required or likely to emerge in different societies. The continuing fallout of the fiscal and economic crises since 2008, in combination with global structural socioeconomic and technological developments, suggest that long-term systemic changes can be anticipated (Norman et al, 2013: 9). For example, among the service areas and economic sectors where it can be predicted with some certainty that demand will grow (particularly in wealthier countries) are social care, health, housing provision and education and training (Mulgan et al, 2007b). Conventional markets often fail to meet these needs adequately and provide these services in sufficient number or quality, as many of those who require them do not possess the necessary resources. Social innovations could play a valuable role in pioneering new models to fund or deliver welfare support in such areas. For example, social innovations have been pioneers of what have been described as 'relational' localised and person-centred forms of welfare provision in place of centralised Fordist bureaucratic models (Cottam, 2013). Unfortunately, the interpersonal contacts and trust upon which such innovations currently depend cannot be sustained beyond a certain scale of operations (Dunbar, 2011), preventing them from extending and expanding their impact (should they even wish to do so). However, technological developments may facilitate new operating models and systems. For example, the development of new distributed trust mechanisms might enable social innovations to overcome this limitation. Some forms of distributed trust system use the transparency of reviews, ratings and accumulated reputation to reassure traders and users that exchanges will be secure and fair. Prominent and successful commercial examples include eBay, Uber and Airbnb. These models are becoming more familiar and accepted, while faith has eroded in some older systems of institutionalised trust, such as confidence in banks, credit rating agencies and many areas of government. In tandem with this, the development of blockchain technology to record transactions and store credit and assets could facilitate social innovation. For example, governments could credit assets to individual or household blockchain accounts, perhaps in the form of a citizen's income, or in recognition of contributions to the community or engaging in socially useful work, as in a Community Allowance (Senscot, 2008; Torry, 2013). This transfer could then be used by recipients to pay for access to the welfare services they need. Potentially, the growth and reliability of distributed trust systems, in combination with blockchain technology, could enable small social innovations to expand their activities without the need to create large, bureaucratic institutionalised trust systems and accounting procedures. This development would resemble the way that the M-Pesa mobile phone money transfer system not only avoided the costs involved in setting up conventional banking institutions (for example, branches and offices) but made a business opportunity of the underdeveloped landline telephone infrastructure in sub-Saharan Africa (Rundle, 2015).

Genuine inventiveness and innovation involves reconceptualising problems and redesigning new responses to them. What is required in order to satisfy growing demands and respond to emerging social issues is not just imaginative micro-level innovations but macro-social transformations. Providing for those unable to afford the welfare and care support they need requires separating supply from effective demand and therefore socialising rather than further marketising or privatising welfare services. In this way, 'Social innovation, based in solidarity and reciprocity, is an alternative to the logic of the market ideology and suggests a different theoretical departure' (Grimm et al, 2013: 448). The most radical and transformational visions of social innovation go beyond offering new ways of delivering welfare services or serving needs after they arise, to develop a different economic system or alternatives to the dominant ethos of contemporary capitalism. Examples of such alternatives might include a renewed and reinvigorated global cooperative movement or an expanded collaborative economy (Williams, 2007; Stokes et al, 2014). This interpretation of social innovation overlaps with such ideas as developing an economics of wellbeing or replacing classical economic models and systems with 'Humanomics' (Layard, 2011; Sedlacek, 2011). This ambitious interpretation of social innovation is implied by some definitions, which describe it as:

> The development and delivery of new ideas and solutions (products, services, models, markets, processes) at different socio-structural levels that intentionally seek to change power relations and improve human capabilities, as well as the processes via which these solutions are carried out. (Nicholls and Ziegler, 2014: 2)

Despite continuing economic problems, this is not the current direction of social and public policy in most societies, and the biggest challenges to this optimistic scenario are not technological but social and attitudinal. The capacity or willingness of the cooperative movement to advance transformational change is questionable: 'throughout their long history co-operatives have been more inclined to foster quiet, evolutionary change than a radical overhaul of the status quo. A co-operative or mutual business exists for its members and their economic and social benefit' (Mazzarol, 2012). Voluntary mutualism does not seem to be a viable basis for large-scale welfare provision; so there will continue to be a need for state intervention and enforcement to meet social needs (Sinclair, 2014).

A further related factor inhibiting the techno–utopian hope that social innovations may become mainstream macro-social institutions through distributed trust systems and blockchain databases is that there is no evident public appetite for conferring credits or welfare entitlements to all of those who need but are currently unable to purchase them.

Distributed trust services must grow to such a scale that existing models cannot ignore them. In commercial systems, this growth can be organic, user-led and bottom-up. However, it is difficult to see how low–income or vulnerable users of social care or income maintenance services could generate sufficient market power to compel a fundamental change in provision. Such a change would have to be led by government for the benefit of such users. But the political leadership this requires would have to build upon a foundation of public support and solidarity, and this is not evident; in fact, in some cases it appears to be weakening (Svallfors, 2012). The possibilities of social innovation (like every other initiative in social and public policy) remain dependent upon public acceptance and political reality. Until there is a secure moral and political foundation for a different form of welfare community, social innovations will remain fascinating but secondary features of the social policy landscape.

References

Adams, D. and Hess, M. (2010) 'Social innovation and why it has policy significance', *The Economic and Labour Relations Review*, 21(2): 139–56.

Akerlof, G. A. and Shiller, R. J (2015) *Phising for phools: The economics of manipulation and deception*, New Haven, CT: Princeton University Press.

Alcock, P. (2005) '"Maximum Feasible Understanding": lessons from previous wars on poverty', *Social Policy & Society*, 4(3): 321–9.

Alpert, D., Hockett, R. C. and Roubini, N. (2011) *The way forward: Moving from the post-bubble, post-bust economy to renewed growth and competitiveness*, Ithaca, NY: Cornell Law Faculty Publications..

Andor, L. (2011) Speech at the launch of the Social Innovation Europe Initiative, Brussels, 16 March. Available from: http://europa.eu/rapid/press-release_SPEECH-11-189_en.htm [accessed 2 November 2016].

Artemis, P. and Sawyer, M. (2004) *Neo-liberal economic policy: Critical essays*, Cheltenham: Edward Elgar.

Arthur, W. Brian (2009) *The nature of technology: What it is and how it evolves*, London: Penguin.

Ayob, N., Teasdale, S. and Fagan, K. (2016) 'How social innovation "came to be": the evolution of a contested concept', *Journal of Social Policy*, 45(4): 635–53.

Baccaro, L. and Howell, C. (2010) 'A common neoliberal trajectory: the transformation of industrial relations in advanced capitalism', *Politics and Society*, 39(4): 521–63.

Baglioni, M. and Brandl, B. (eds) (2011) *Changing labour relations: Between path dependency and global trends*, Frankfurt: Peter Lang.

Baglioni, S., della Porta, D. and Graziano, P. (2008) 'The contentious politics of unemployment: the Italian case in comparative perspective', *European Journal of Political Research*, 47(6): 827–51.

Baglioni, S., De Pieri, B. and Tallarico, T. (2016) 'Surplus food recovery and food aid: the pivotal role of non-profit organisations: insights from Italy and Germany', *Voluntas: International Journal of Voluntary and Non-Profit Organizations*, DOI: 10.1007/s11266-016-9746-8

Baglioni, S., Calò, F., Garrone, P. and Molteni, M. (eds) (2017) *Foodsaving in Europe: At the Crossroad of social innovation*, Basingstoke: Palgrave Macmillan.

Baldwin, P. (1990) *The politics of social solidarity: Class bases of the European welfare state, 1875–1975*, Cambridge: Cambridge University Press.

Barroso, J. M. (2011) *Europe leading social innovation*, Brussels: Social Innovation Europe Initiative.

Bason, C. (2010) *Leading public sector innovation: Co-creating for a better society*, Bristol: Policy Press.

Bateman, M. (2010) *Why doesn't microfinance work? The destructive rise of neoliberalism*, London: Zed Books.

Bateson, G. (1972) *Steps to an ecology of mind*, San Francisco, CA: Chandler.

BCFN (2012) *Food waste: Causes, impacts and proposal*, Milan: Codice Edizioni.

Benneworth, P., Amanatidou, E., Edwards Schachter, M. and Gulbrandsen, M. (2014) *Social innovation futures: Beyond policy panacea and conceptual ambiguity*. Position paper for the EU-SPRI Forum. Available from: http://doc.utwente.nl/94038/1/benneworth%20paper%20H.pdf [accessed 31 October 2016].

BEPA (2010) *Empowering people, driving change: Social innovation in the European Union*, Luxembourg: Bureau of European Policy Advisers.

Beresford, P. and Carr, S. (eds) (2012) *Social care, service users and user involvement*, London: Jessica Kingsley Publishers.

Billis, D. (ed) (2010) *Hybrid organizations and the third sector: Challenges for practice, theory and policy*, Basingstoke: Palgrave Macmillan.

BIO by Deloitte (2014) *Comparative study on EU member states' legislation and practices on food donation*, Brussels: European Economic and Social Committee.

Bishop, M. and Green, M. (2008) *Philanthrocapitalism: How the rich can save the world and why we should let them*, London: Bloomsbury.

Boadu, P., Gluns, D., Rentzsch, C., Walter, A. and Zimmer, A. (2014) 'Münster', in B. Ewert, A. Evers and T. Brandsen (eds) *Social innovations for social cohesion: Transnational patterns and approaches from 20 European cities*, Liege: EMES, pp 131–56. Available from: www.wilcoproject.eu/downloads/WILCO-project-eReader.pdf [accessed 20 September 2017].

Bonifacio, M. (2014) 'Social innovation: a novel policy stream or a policy compromise? An EU perspective', *European Review*, 22(1): 145–69.

Bornstein, D. (2004) *How to change the world: Social entrepreneurs and the power of ideas*, Oxford: Oxford University Press.

Borzaga, C. and Bodini, C. (2012) *What to make of social innovation? Towards a framework for policy development*, Trento: Euricse.

Borzaga, C. and Defourny, J. (eds) (2001) *The emergence of social enterprise*, London: Routledge.

Brandsen, T., Evers, A., Cattacin, S. and Zimmer, A. (2016) 'Social innovation: a sympathetic and critical interpretation', in T. Brandsen, S. Cattacin, A. Evers, and A. Zimmer (eds) *Social innovations in the urban context*, London: Springer, pp 3–18.

Broersma, F., Fledderus, J. and Brandsen, T. (2014) 'Nijmegen', in B. Ewert, A. Evers and T. Brandsen (eds) *Social innovations for social cohesion: Transnational patterns and approaches from 20 European cities*, Liege: EMES European Research Network, pp 223–42. Available from: www.wilcoproject.eu/downloads/WILCO-project-eReader. pdf [accessed 20 September 2017].

Brookes, N., Kendall, J. and Mitton, L. (2014) 'Birmingham', in B. Ewert, A. Evers and T. Brandsen (eds) *Social innovations for social cohesion: Transnational patterns and approaches from 20 European cities*, Liege: EMES European Research Network, pp 381–96. Available from: www.wilcoproject.eu/downloads/WILCO-project-eReader. pdf [accessed 20 September 2017].

Brown, T. and Wyatt, J. (2010) 'Design thinking for social innovation', *Stanford Social Innovation Review*, (Winter). Available from: https://ssir. org/articles/entry/design_thinking_for_social_innovation [accessed 20 September 2017].

Bunt, L. and Harris, M. (2010) *Mass localism: A way to help small communities solve big social challenges*, London: NESTA.

Burke, E. (1790) *Reflections on the revolution in France and on the proceedings in certain societies in London relative to that event in a letter intended to have been sent to gentleman in Paris.* Available from: http://socserv2.mcmaster.ca/~econ/ugcm/3ll3/burke/revfrance. pdf [accessed 2 November 2016].

Carr, R. (2015) *Commercial councils: The rise of entrepreneurialism in local government.* Available from: www.localis.org.uk/research/ commercial-councils-the-rise-of-entrepreneurialism-in-local-government/ [accessed 20 September 2017].

Casebourne, L. (2013) 'Making it work: why we need innovation to tackle worklessness', *Working Brief*, Spring: 20–26, https://www2. learningandwork.org.uk/sites/default/files/working_brief_back_ issues/WB_Spring%202013_print.pdf

Castel, R. (2004) *L'insécurité sociale. Qu'est-ce qu'être protégé?* Paris: Seuil.

Castells, M. (1996) *The rise of the network society*, Cambridge: Blackwell.

Castles, F. G. (ed) (1993) *Families of nations: Patterns of public policy in Western democracies*, Aldershot: Dartmouth.

Castles, F. G. (2009) 'What welfare states do: a disaggregated expenditure approach', *Journal of Social Policy*, 38(1): 45–62.

Caulier-Grice, J., Davies, A., Patrick, R. and Norman, W. (2012) *Defining social innovation: part one of Social Innovation Overview: a deliverable of the project: 'the theoretical, empirical and policy foundations for building social innovation in Europe'*, Brussels: European Commission, DG Research.

Chalmers, D. (2012) 'Social innovation: an exploration of the barriers faced by innovating organizations in the social economy', *Local Economy*, 28(1): 17–34.

Chang, H-J. (2014) *Economics: The user's guide*, London: Pelican.

Chase, R. (2015) Peers inc: *How people and platforms are inventing the collaborative economy and reinventing capitalism*, New York: PublicAffairs.

Chesbrough, H. W. (2003) *Open innovation: The new imperative for creating and profiting from technology*, Cambridge, MA: Harvard Business School Press.

Conceição, P. and Mendoza, R. (2009) 'Anatomy of the global food crisis', *Third World Quarterly*, 30(6): 1159–82.

Conger, S. (1996) 'Social inventions', *The Innovation Journal: The Public Sector Innovation Journal*, 1 (2). Available from: www.innovation.cc/discussion-papers/social_invention1995sstije_v1i2a1.pdf

Coqblin, A. and Fraisse, L. (2014) 'Nantes', in B. Ewert, A. Evers and T. Brandsen (eds) *Social innovations for social cohesion: Transnational patterns and approaches from 20 European cities*, Liege: EMES European Research Network, pp 89–108. Available from: www.wilcoproject.eu/downloads/WILCO-project-eReader.pdf [accessed 20 September 2017].

Costa, M. (2017) 'Social return on investment, including elements on cost-benefit analysis', in B. Greve (ed) *Handbook of social policy evaluation*, Cheltenham: Edward Elgar, pp 57–76.

Cottam, H. (2013) 'From transactional welfare to relational welfare', *New Start*, (6 March). Available from: https://newstartmag.co.uk/articles/relational-welfare/ [accessed 2 November 2016].

Cremin, C. (2010) 'Never employable enough: the (im)possibility of satisfying the boss's desire', *Organization*, 17(2): 131–49.

Cumming, L. (2008) *To guide the human puppet: Behavioural economics, public policy and public service contracting*, Hook: The Serco Institute.

Dahrendorf, R. (1988) *The modern social conflict: An essay on the politics of liberty*, London: Weidenfeld and Nicolson.

Daigneault, P-M. (2014) 'Reassessing the concept of policy paradigm: aligning ontology and methodology in policy studies', *Journal of European Public Policy*, 21(3): 453–69.

David, P. A. (1985) 'Clio and the economics of QWERTY', *American Economic Review* (Papers and Proceedings), 75(2): 332–7.

Dawson, P. and Daniel, L. (2010) 'Understanding social innovation: a provisional framework', *International Journal of Technology Management*, 51(1): 9–12.

Defourny, J. and Nyssens, M. (2010) 'Conceptions of social enterprise and social entrepreneurship in Europe and the United States: convergences and divergences', *Journal of Social Entrepreneurship*, 1(1): 32–53.

della Porta, D., Hänninen, S., Siisiäinen, M. and Silvasti, T. (2015) *The new social division: Making and unmaking precarity*, Basingstoke: Palgrave Macmillan.

Department for Business, Innovation and Skills (2014) *Innovation, research and growth: Innovation Report 2014*, London: Department for Business, Innovation and Skills.

de Tocqueville, A. (2010) *Democracy in America* (edited by E. Nolla, translated by J. T. Schleifer), Indianapolis, IN: Liberty Fund (originally published 1835). Available from: http://classiques.uqac.ca/classiques/De_tocqueville_alexis/democracy_in_america_historical_critical_ed/democracy_in_america_vol_2.pdf [accessed 2 November 2016].

De Vries, H., Bekkers, V. and Trummers, L. (2014) 'Innovation in the public sector: a systematic review and future research agenda', Speyer: EGPA Conference. Available from: http://www.lipse.org/userfiles/uploads/Innovation%20in%20the%20public%20sector%20-%20De%20Vries%20Bekkers%20Tummers.pdf [accessed 31 October 2016].

Diamond, J. (2013) *The world until yesterday: What can we learn from traditional societies?* London: Penguin.

Dowler, E. (1998) 'Food poverty and food policy', *IDS Bulletin*, 29(1): 58–65.

Drayton, B. (2004) *Leading social entrepreneurs changing the world.* London: Ashoka.

Duffy, P. A., Hallmark, G. G., Molnar, J., Claxton, L., Bailey, C. and Mikloucich, S. (2002) 'Food security of low-income single parents in East Alabama: use of private and public programs in the age of welfare reform', *Southern Rural Sociology*, 18(1): 48–81.

Dunbar, R. (2011) *How many friends does one person need?: Dunbar's number and other evolutionary quirks.* London: Faber & Faber.

Duncan Smith, I. (2012) *Social justice: Transforming lives*, speech delivered on 13 March 2012, London: Department for Work and Pensions Available from: www.gov.uk/government/speeches/social-justice-transforming-lives [accessed 2 November 2016].

Durie, R., Wyatt K. and Stuteley, H. (2004) 'Community regeneration and complexity', in D. Kernick (ed) *Complexity and healthcare organization: A view from the street*, Abingdon: Radcliffe Medical Press, pp 279–87.

Edelman, R. (2015) 'Earning the right to innovate'. Available from: www.edelman.com/p/6-a-m/earning-the-right-to-innovate [accessed 2 November 2016].

Edmiston, D. (2015) EU public policy, social innovation and marginalisation: Reconciling ambitions with policy instruments, CRESSI Working Paper Series No. 18/2015, Oxford: Oxford University.

El Sistema (no date) 'Guiding principles', El Sistema USA. Available from: www.elsistemausa.org/guiding-principles.htm.

Engler-Stringer, R. and Berenbaum, S. (2007) 'Exploring food security with collective kitchens participants in three Canadian cities', *Quality Health Research*, 17(1): 75–84.

Esping-Andersen, G. (1991) *The three worlds of welfare capitalism*, Cambridge: Polity.

Etzioni, A. (1995) *The spirit of community: Rights, responsibilities and the communitarian agenda*, London: Fontana.

European Commission (2009) 'President Barroso discusses how to boost "social innovation"' (press release), Brussels: European Commission.

European Commission (2010) *Europe 2020 flagship initiative innovation union*. Brussels: European Commission.

European Commission (2013a) *Guide to social innovation*. Luxembourg: European Commission DG Regional and Urban Policy, Social Affairs and Inclusion.

European Commission (2013b) *Social economy and social entrepreneurship*, Social Europe Guide, Vol 4, Luxembourg: Publications Office of the European Union.

Eurostat (2015a) 'Census data 2011', Brussels: Eurostat. Available from: http://ec.europa.eu/eurostat/web/population-and-housing-census/census-data/database [accessed 21 September 2017].

Eurostat (2015b) 'Unemployment Statistics', Brussels: Eurostat, http://ec.europa.eu/eurostat/statistics-explained/index.php/Unemployment_statistics [accessed 30 October 2017].

Eurostat (2017) 'Migration and migrant population statistics', Brussels: Eurostat. Available from: http://ec.europa.eu/eurostat/statistics-explained/index.php/Migration_and_migrant_population_statistics [accessed 7 November 2017].

Evers, A., Ewert, B. and Brandsen, T. (eds) (2014) *Social innovations for social cohesion: Transnational patterns and approaches from 20 European cities*, Liege: WILCO. Available from: www.wilcoproject.eu/downloads/WILCO-project-eReader.pdf [accessed 2 November 2016].

Ewert, B. and Evers, A. (2014) 'Friedrichshaein-Kreuzberg', in B. Ewert, A. Evers and T. Brandsen (eds) *Social innovations for social cohesion: Transnational patterns and approaches from 20 European cities*, Liege: WILCO, 109–30. Available from: www.wilcoproject.eu/downloads/WILCO-project-eReader.pdf [accessed 2 November 2016].FAO (2009) *The state of food insecurity in the world*, Rome: Food and Agricultural Organization.

FAO (2011) *Global food losses and food waste: Extent, causes and prevention*, Rome: Food and Agricultural Organization.

Faranda, I. (2013) 'Condomini per la vita indipendente: Ghetto o opportunità?' (unpublished MA dissertation), Bologna: University of Bologna.

Farnsworth, K. (2004) *Corporate power and social policy*, Bristol: Policy Press.

Farnsworth, K. (2012) *Social versus corporate welfare*, Basingstoke: Palgrave Macmillan.

Ferrara, I. and Missios, P. (2012) 'A cross-country study of household waste prevention and recycling: assessing the effectiveness of policy instruments', *Land Economics,* 88(4): 710–44.

Ferrera, M. (2008) *Il fattore D. Perché il lavoro delle donne farà crescere l'Italia*, Milan: Mondadori.

Finn, S. M. (2011) 'A public–private initiative to reduce food waste: a framework for local communities', *Graduate Studies Journal of Organizational Dynamics*, 1(1) Article 3.

Florida, R. (2002) *The rise of the creative class*, New York: Basic Books.

Fraisse, L. (2014) 'Lille' in B. Ewert, A. Evers and T. Brandsen (eds) *Social innovations for social cohesion: Transnational patterns and approaches from 20 European cities*, Liege: WILCO, 67–88. Available from: www.wilcoproject.eu/downloads/WILCO-project-eReader.pdf [accessed 2 November 2016].

Frane, A. and Westland, H. (eds) (2013) *Innovations in socio-cultural context*, London: Routledge.

Franz, H-W., Hochgerner, J. and Howaldt J. (2012) 'Challenge social innovation: an introduction', in H-W. Franz, J. Hochgerner and J. Howaldt (eds) *Challenge social innovation: Potentials for business, social entrepreneurship, welfare and civil society*, Berlin: Springer, pp 1–16.

Friel, S. and Conlon, C. (2004) *Food poverty and policy*, Dublin: Combat Poverty Agency, Crosscare and the Society of St Vincent de Paul. Available from: www.combatpoverty.ie/publications/FoodPovertyAndPolicy_2004.pdf [accessed 21 September 2017].

Frey C. B. and Osborne, M. (2013) *The future of employment: How susceptible are jobs to computerisation?* Oxford: Martin Programme on the Impacts of Future Technology.

Friedli, L. (2011) 'Always look on the bright side: the rise of assets-based approaches in Scotland', *Scottish Anti-Poverty Review*, 14 (Winter 2011/12): 11–15.

Furlong, A. and Cartmel, F. (2004) *Vulnerable young men in fragile labour markets: Employment, unemployment and the search for long-term security*, York: Joseph Rowntree Foundation.

Galbraith, J. K. (1997) *The* good society: *The humane agenda*, New York: Houghton Mifflin.

Garrone, P., Melacini, M. and Perego, A. (2014a) 'Opening the black box of food waste reduction', *Food Policy,* 46 (issue C): 129–39.

Garrone, P., Melacini, M. and Perego, A. (2014b) 'Surplus food recovery and donation in Italy: the upstream process', *British Food Journal,* 116(9): 1460–77.

Garthwaite, K. (2016) *Hunger pains: Life inside foodbank Britain*, Bristol: Policy Press.

Gartner (n.d.) 'Gartner Hype Cycle'. Available from: www.gartner.com/technology/research/methodologies/hype-cycle.jsp

Gerometta, J., Häussermann, H. and Longo, G. (2005) 'Social innovation and civil society in urban governance: strategies for an inclusive city', *Urban Studies*, 42(11): 2007–21.

Gerth, H. H. and Mills, C. W. (1948) 'Introduction: the man and his work', in H. H. Gerth and C. W. Mills (eds) *From Max Weber: Essays in sociology*, London: Routledge and Kegan Paul, pp 3–75.

Giddens, A. (1971) *Capitalism and modern social theory*, Cambridge: Cambridge University Press.

Giddens, A. (1991) *Modernity and self-identity: Self and society in the late modern age*, Cambridge: Polity.

Godin, B. (2012) *Social innovation: Utopias of innovation from c. 1830 to the present*, Project on the Intellectual History of Innovation Working Paper No. 11, Montreal: INRS.

Godin, B. (2015) *Innovation contested: The idea of innovation over the centuries*, London: Routledge.

Govindarajan, V. and Trimble, C. (2012) *Reverse innovation: Create far from home, win everywhere*, Cambridge, MA: Harvard Business Review Press.

Greenhalgh, T., Robert G., Macfarlane, F., Bate, P. and Kyriakidou, O. (2004) 'Diffusion of innovations in service organizations: systematic review andrecommendations', *The Milbank Quarterly*, 82(4): 1–37.

Gregory, P. J., Ingram, J. S. I. and Brklacich, M. (2005) 'Climate change and food security', *Philosophical Transactions of the Royal Society*, 360(1463): 2139–48.

Gretzinger, S., Fietze, S. and Matisake, W. (2015) 'Innovation networks: editorial', *Management Review*, 26(2): 81–2.

Grimm, R., Fox, C., Baines, S. and Albertson, K. (2013) 'Social innovation: an answer to contemporary societal challenges? Locating the concept in theory and practice', *Innovation: The European Journal of Social Science Research*, 26(4): 436–55.

Habermas, J. (1973) *Legitimation crisis* (translated by T. McCarthy), London: Heinemann.

Hämäläinen, T. J. and Heiskala, R. (eds) (2007*) Social innovations, institutional change and economic performance: Making sense of structural adjustment processes in industrial sectors, regions and societies*, Cheltenham: Edward Elgar.

Harkins, C. and Egan, J. (2012) *The role of participatory budgeting in promoting localism and mobilising community assets: But where next for participatory budgeting in Scotland?* Glasgow: Glasgow Centre for Population Health.

Harris, R. (2005) *The semantics of science*, London: Continuum.

Harris, M. and Albury, D. (2009) *The innovation imperative: Why radical innovation is needed to reinvent public services for the recession and beyond*, London: NESTA.

Hartley, J. (2014) 'New development: eight and a half propositions to stimulate frugal innovation', *Public Money &Management*, 34(3): 227–32.

Hills, J. (2014) *Good times, bad times: The welfare myth of them and us*, Bristol: Policy Press.

Hobsbawm, E. (1994) *The age of extremes: The short twentieth century, 1914–1991*, London: Michael Joseph.

Howaldt, J. and Schwarz, M. (2010) *Social innovation: Concepts, research fields and international trends,* Dortmund: Sozialforschungsstelle Dortmund.

IFRC (2013) *Think differently: Humanitarian impacts of the economic crisis in Europe,* Geneva: International Federation of Red Cross and Red Crescent Societies. Available from: www.ifrc.org/PageFiles/134339/1260300-Economic%20crisis%20Report_EN_LR.pdf [accessed 21 September 2017].

Jenson, J. and Harrison, D. (2013) *Social innovation research in the European Union: Approaches, findings and future directions, policy review,* Luxembourg: European Union.

Jessop, B. (1994) 'The transition to post-Fordism and the Schumpeterian workfare state', in R. Burrows and B. Loader (eds) *Towards a post-Fordist welfare state?* Abingdon: Routledge, pp 13–37.

Jha, M. K. (2009) 'Food security in perspective: the significance of social action', *Community Development Journal,* 44(3): 351–66.

Kenyon, N. (2015) 'The triumph of a musical adventure', *New York Review of Books*, 24 September.

Keynes, J.M. (1926) 'Liberalism and labour in England', *New Republic*, 3 March. Available from: https://newrepublic.com/article/77341/liberalism-and-labor-in-england [accessed 21st October 2017].

Kitschelt, H.P. (1986) 'Political opportunity structures and political orotest: anti-nuclear movements in four democracies', *British Journal of Political Science*, 16(1): 57–85.

Kupchan, C. A. (2012) 'The democratic malaise: globalization and the threat to the West', *Foreign Affairs*, 91 (Jan/Feb): 62–7.

Lang, T. and Barling, D. (2012) 'Food security and food sustainability: reformulating the debate', *The Geographical Journal,* 178(4): 313–26.

Layard, R. (2011) Happiness: Lessons from a new science. (2nd edn). London: Penguin.

Leadbeater, C. and Wong, A. (2010) *Learning from the extremes*, San Jose: Cisco Systems. Available from: www.cisco.com/c/dam/en_us/about/citizenship/socio-economic/docs/LearningfromExtremes_WhitePaper.pdf [accessed 2 November 2016].

Lindström, B. and Eriksson, M. (2005) 'Salutogenesis', *Journal of Epidemiology and Community Health*, 59(6): 440–2. Available from: http://jech.bmj.com/content/59/6/440 [accessed 21 September 2017].

Lupton, R. (2003) *Poverty street: The dynamics of neighbourhood decline and renewal*, London: LSE Centre for Analysis of Social Exclusion.

Lynn, L. (1997) 'Innovation and the public interest: insights from the private sector', in A. Altchuler and R. Behn. (eds) *Innovation in American Government*, Washington, DC: Brookings Institution, pp 83–104.

MacDonald, R. (2011) 'Youth transitions, unemployment and underemployment: plus ça change, plus c'est la même chose?', *Journal of Sociology* 47(4): 427–4.

MacDonald, R. and Marsh, J. (2005) *Disconnected youth?: Growing up in Britain's poor neighbourhoods*, Basingstoke: Palgrave Macmillan.

MacDonald, R., Shildrick, T., Webster, C. and Simpson, D. (2005) 'Growing up in poor neighbourhoods: the significance of class and place in the extended transitions of "socially excluded" young adults', *Sociology* 39(5): 873–91.

McHugh, N., Sinclair, S., Roy, M., Huckfield, L. and Donaldson, C. (2013) 'Social impact bonds: a wolf in sheep's clothing?' *Journal of Poverty and Social Justice*, 21(3): 247–57.

McKinlay J.B. (1975) 'A case for refocusing upstream: the political economy of illness', in A. Enlow (ed) *Behavioral Aspects of Prevention*, Dallas: American Heart Association, pp 9–25.

Madrick, J. (2014). 'Innovation: the government was crucial after all', *The New York Review of Books,* LXI (7), 24 April.

Maino, F., Lodi Rizzini, C. and Bandera, L. (2016) *Povertà alimentare in Italia: le risposte del secondo welfare*, Bologna: il Mulino.

Mason, P. (2011) *Why it's all kicking off everywhere: The new global revolutions*, London: Verso.

Mavra, L. (2011) *Growing social enterprise: Research into social replication*, London: Social Enterprise Coalition.

Mazzarol, T. (2012) 'Co-operatives and social enterprise: are they a replacement for mainstream capitalism?' *The Conversation*, 4 November.

Mazzucato, M. (2013) *The entrepreneurial state: Debunking public vs. private sector myths*, London: Anthem Press.

Membretti, A. (2007) 'Building citizenship as an innovative service', *European Urban and Regional Studies*, 14(3): 252–63.

Mendelson, M. (2007) 'Asset-based social programs: a critical analysis of current initiatives', OECD seminar *Life Risks, Life Course and Social Policy*, Paris, 31 May – 1 June. Available from: www.oecd.org/els/public-pensions/38718611.pdf [accessed 2 November 2016].

Mishra, R. (1984) *The welfare state in crisis: Social thought and social change*, Brighton: Wheatsheaf.

Montgomery, T. (2013) *Implementing a Scottish social innovation strategy: Support from the European Regional Development Fund*, Edinburgh: Scottish Government. Available from: www.gov.scot/Resource/0043/00434672.pdf [accessed 2 November 2016].

Montgomery, T., Mazzei, M., Baglioni, S. and Sinclair, S. (2017) 'Who cares? The social care sector and the future of youth employment', *Policy and Politics*, 45(3): 413–29.

Mooney, G. and Scott, G. (2016) 'Welfare, equality and social justice: Scottish independence and the dominant imaginings of the "new" Scotland', *Ethics and Social Welfare*, 10(3): 239–51.

Moore, M. and Hartley, J. (2008) 'Innovations in governance', *Public Management Review*, 10(1): 3–20.

Moore, M-L. and Westley, F. R. (2011) 'Public sector policy and strategies for facilitating social innovation', Horizons Centre for International Governance Innovation. Available from: https://uwaterloo.ca/waterloo-institute-for-social-innovation-and-resilience/sites/ca.waterloo-institute-for-social-innovation-and-resilience/files/uploads/files/public_sector_policy.pdf [accessed 2 November 2016].

Moran, M. (2014) 'Will more business-like social enterprises improve care?' *The Conversation*, 18 March. Available from: http://theconversation.com/will-more-business-like-social-enterprises-improve-care-23643 [accessed 2 November 2016].

Morel, N., Palier, B. and Palme, J. (2012) 'Beyond the welfare state as we know it?' in N. Morel, B. Palier and J. Palme (eds). *Towards a social investment welfare state? Ideas, policies and challenges*, Bristol: Policy Press, pp 1–30.

Moretti, E. (2012) *The new geography of jobs*, New York: Houghton Mifflin Harcourt.

Moulaert, F. (2009) 'Social innovation: institutionally embedded, territorially (re)produced', in D. MacCallam et al (eds) *Social innovation and territorial development*, Farnham: Ashgate, pp 11–24.

Moulaert, F., Martinelli, F., Swyngedouw, E. and Gonzalez, S. (2005) 'Towards alternative model(s) of local innovation', *Urban Studies*, 42(11): 1969–90.

Mulgan, G. (2007) *Ready or not: Taking innovation in the public sector seriously*, London: NESTA.

Mulgan, G., Ali, R., Halkett, R. and Sanders, B. (2007a) *In and out of synch: The challenge of growing social innovations,* London: NESTA.

Mulgan, G., Tucker, S., Ali, R. and Sanders, B. (2007b) *Social innovation: What it is, why it matters and how it can be accelerated*, Oxford: Said Business School.

Murray, R., Caulier-Grice, J. and Mulgan, G. (2010) *Open book of social innovation*, London: NESTA.

Nasar, S. (2012) *Grand pursuit: The story of the people who made modern economics*, London: Fourth Estate.

Naughton, J. (2015) 'We are ignoring the new machine age at our peril', *The Observer*, 17 May.

NESTA (2007) *Innovation in response to social challenges*, London: NESTA.

New Internationalist (nd) 'Microcredit and Grameen Bank'. Available from: https://newint.org/books/reference/world-development/case-studies/poverty-microcredit-grameen-bank/ [accessed 22 September 2017].

Nicholls, A. (ed) (2006) *Social entrepreneurship: New models of sustainable social change*, Oxford: Oxford University Press.

Nicholls, A. and Murdock, A. (eds) (2012) *Social innovation: Blurring boundaries to reconfigure markets*, Basingstoke: Palgrave Macmillan.

Nicholls, A. and Ziegler, R. (2014) 'An extended social grid model for the study of marginalisation processes and social innovation, in B. Houghton Budd, C. W. M. Naastepad and C. Van Beers (eds) *Report on institutions, social innovation and system dynamics from the perspective of the marginalised: A deliverable of the project 'Creating Economic Space for Social Innovation'* (CRESSI), Brussels: European Commission, DG Research and Innovation, 7th Framework Programme Available from: www.sbs.ox.ac.uk/sites/default/files/research-projects/CRESSI/docs/CRESSI_Working_Paper_2_D1.1_Chp2_18Nov2014.pdf [accessed 21 October 2017].

Nordfeldt, M. and Carrigan, A. (2014) 'Stokholm', in B. Ewert, A. Evers and T. Brandsen (eds) *Social innovations for social cohesion: Transnational patterns and approaches from 20 European cities*, Liege: WILCO, 317–34. Available from: www.wilcoproject.eu/downloads/WILCO-project-eReader.pdf [accessed 2 November 2016].

Norman, W., Russell, C., Clarke, K. and Mackin, D. (2013) *Growing social innovation in Northern Ireland*, London: Young Foundation.

Northern Ireland Executive (2014) *Innovation strategy for Northern Ireland, 2014–2025*, Belfast: Northern Ireland Executive, Department for the Economy.

Nosko, A. and Széger, K. (2013) *Active citizenship can change your country for the better*, Open Society Foundation, 25 February. Available from: www.opensocietyfoundations.org/voices/active-citizenship-can-change-your-country-better [accessed 2 November 2016]

O'Connor, J. (1979) *The fiscal crisis of the state*, New Brunswick, NJ: Transaction.

OECD (2012) *Looking to 2060: Long-term global growth prospects*, Paris: OECD.

OECD (2014) *Social expenditure update*, Paris: OECD.

O'Hara, M. (2015) *Austerity bites: A journey to the sharp end of cuts in the UK*, Bristol: Policy Press.

Okpara, J. O. and Halkias, D. (2011) 'Social entrepreneurship: an overview of its theoretical evolution and proposed research model', *International Journal of Social Entrepreneurship and Innovation*, 1(1): 4–20.

Orton, M. (2015) *Something's not right: Insecurity and an anxious nation*, London: Compass.

Parfitt, J., Barthel, M. and Macnaughton, S. (2010) 'Food waste within food supply chains: quantification and potential for change to 2050', *Philosophical Transactions of the Royal Society B*, 365(1554): 3065–81.

Paugam, S. (2000) *Le salarié de la précarité*, Paris: Presses Universitaires de France.

Peck, J. and Theodore, N. (2000) 'Beyond "employability"', *Cambridge Journal of Economics*, 24(6): 729–49.

Persson, T., and Hafen, N. (2014) *Social enterprise, social entrepreunership and social innovation in Sweden: A national report.* Available from: www.fp7-efeseiis.eu/national-report-sweden [accessed 22 September 2017].

Phills, J. A., Deiglmeier, K. and Miller, D. T. (2008) 'Rediscovering social innovation', *Stanford Social Innovation Review*, 6 (Fall).

Pierson, P. (2000) 'Increasing returns: path dependence and the study of politics', *American Political Science Review*, 94(2): 251–67.

Pol, E. and Ville, S. (2009) 'Social innovation: buzz word or enduring term?' *Journal of Socio-Economics*, 38: 878–85.

Pollitt, C. and Hupe, P. (2011) 'Talking about government: the role of magic concepts', *Public Management Review*, 13(5): 641–58.

Porter, M. E. and Kramer, M. R. (2011) 'Creating shared value', *Harvard Business Review*, (Jan/Feb).

Portes, A. and Landolt, P. (1996) 'The downside of social capital', *The American Prospect*, 7(26): 18–21.

Powell, M. (ed.) (2007) *Understanding the mixed economy of welfare*, Bristol: Policy Press.

Pugliese, E. (1993) *Sociologia della disoccupazione*, Bologna: il Mulino.

Ravitch, D. (2012) 'How, and how not, to improve the schools', *New York Review of Books*, 22 March. Available from: www.nybooks.com/articles/2012/03/22/how-and-how-not-improve-schools [accessed 22 September 2017].

Reinstaller, A. (2013) *An evolutionary view on social innovation and the process of economic change*, Vienna: WWWforEurope.

Riches, G. (2002) 'Food banks and food security: welfare reform, human rights and social policy: lessons from Canada?' *Social Policy and Administration,* 36(6): 648–63.

Ridley-Duff, R. and Bull, M. (2011). *Understanding social enterprise: Theory and practice*, London: Sage.

Rigby, J. and Hayden, J. (2013) 'Are IPR and open innovation good for each other? Surely an open and shut case?' in D. Cox and J. Rigby (eds) *Innovation policy challenges for the 21st century*, London: Routledge, pp 89–109.

Roberts, Y. (2008) 'New ways of doing', *The Guardian*, 11 August.

Roodman, D. (2012) 'Microcredit doesn't end poverty, despite the hype', *Washington Post*, 8 March.

Room, G. (1995) *Beyond the threshold: The measurement and analysis of social exclusion*, Bristol: Polity Press.

RQIS (2011) *Quebec Declaration on Social Innovation*, Quebec: University of Quebec, Le Réseau Québecois en Innovation Sociale. Available from: www.rqis.org/wp-content/uploads/2014/08/Quebec-Declaration-on-Social-Innovation.pdf [accessed 31 October 2016].

Ruddat, C. and Schönauer, A-L. (2014) 'New players on crowded playing fields: the institutional embeddedness of social innovation in Germany', *Social Policy & Society*, 13(3): 445–56.

Runde, D. (2015) 'M-Pesa and the rise of the global mobile money market', *Forbes*, 12 August. Available from: www.forbes.com/sites/danielrunde/2015/08/12/m-pesa-and-the-rise-of-the-global-mobile-money-market/#79e5089723f5 [accessed 22 September 2017].

Ryan, W. (1971) *Blaming the victim*, London: Pantheon.

Sahlin, K. and Wedlin, L. (2008) 'Circulating ideas: imitation, translation and editing', in R. Greenwood, C. Oliver, K. Sahlin and R. Suddaby (eds) *The SAGE handbook of organizational institutionalism*, London: Sage, pp 218–42.

Sandel, M. J. (2009) *Justice: What's the right thing to do?* London: Penguin.

Sandel, M. (2010) *Liberalism and the limits of justice* (2nd edn), Cambridge: Cambridge University Press.

Sarasvathy, S. D. and Venkataraman, S. (2011) 'Entrepreneurship as method: open questions for an entrepreneurial future', *Entrepreneurship Theory and Practice*, 35(1): 113–35.

Scottish Government (2010) *Health in Scotland 2009, time for change: Annual report of the Chief Medical Officer*, Edinburgh: Scottish Government.

Schumpeter, J. (1976) *Capitalism, socialism and democracy*, London: Routledge (originally published 1942).

Schumpeter, J. (2004) *Theory of economic development*, New York: Transaction Publishers (originally published 1911).

Schneider, F. (2012) 'The evolution of food donation with respect to waste prevention', *Waste Management*, 33(3): 755–63.

Sedlacek, T. (2011) *Economics of good and evil: The quest for economic meaning from Gilgamesh to Wall Street*, Oxford: Oxford University Press.

Seelos, C. and Mair, J. (2005) 'Social entrepreneurship: creating new business models to serve the poor', *Business Horizons*, 48(3): 241–6.

Sen, A. K. (1985) *Commodities and capabilities*, Amsterdam: Elsevier.

Senscot (2008) 'Community Allowance Briefing', 2 September. Available from: www.senscot.net/view_news.php?viewid=7557 [accessed 2 November 2016].

Seyfang, G. and Smith, A. (2007) 'Grassroots innovations for sustainable development: towards a new research agenda', *Environmental Politics*, 16(4): 584–603.

Shakespeare, T. (2013) *Disability rights and wrongs revisited*, London: Routledge.

Sherry, E., and O'May, F. (2013) 'Exploring the impact of sport participation in the Homeless World Cup on individuals with substance abuse or mental health disorders', *Journal of Sport for Development*, 1(2): 17–25

Shildrick, T. A., MacDonald, R., Webster, C. and Garthwaite, K., (2012) *Poverty and insecurity: Life in low-pay, no-pay Britain*, Bristol: Policy Press.

Sinfield, A. (2004) 'Upstream thinking', *Policy World* (Autumn). Available from: www.social-policy.org.uk/wordpress/wp-content/uploads/2012/09/PolicyWorld_Aut04.pdf [accessed 22 September 2017].

Sinclair, S. (2014) 'Credit union modernisation and the limits of voluntarism', *Policy & Politics,* 42(3): 403–19.

Sinclair, S. (2016) *Introduction to social policy analysis: Illuminating welfare*, Bristol: Policy Press.

Sinclair, S. and Baglioni, S. (2014) 'Social innovation and social policy: promises and risks', *Social Policy and Society*, 13(3): 469–76.

Sinclair, S., McHugh, N., Huckfield, L., Roy, M. and Donaldson, C. (2014) 'Social impact bonds: shifting the boundaries of sitizenship', in K. Farnsworth et al (eds) *Social policy review 26: Analysis and debate in social policy*, Bristol: Policy Press, pp 119–36.

Sisson, A. (2011) *The next wave of innovation: Five areas that could pull the UK clear of recession*, Big Innovation Centre.

SIX and Young Foundation (2010) *Study on social innovation*. Bureau of European Policy Advisors. Available from: https://youngfoundation.org/wp-content/uploads/2012/10/Study-on-Social-Innovation-for-the-Bureau-of-European-Policy-Advisors-March-2010.pdf [Accessed 21 October 2017]

Smiles. S. (1996) *Self-help: With illustrations of conduct and perseverance*, London: Institute of Economic Affairs.

Smith, K. (2013) *Beyond evidence-based policy in public health: The interplay of ideas*, Basingstoke: Palgrave Macmillan.

Spear, S. and Moss, E. (2015) 'Social inclusion', *Environmental Health News*, May: 16–18.

Spector, M. and Kitsuse, J. I. (1987) *Constructing social problems*, New York: Aldine de Gruyter.

Spicker, P. (1988) *Principles of social welfare: An introduction to thinking about the welfare state*, London: Routledge.

Spreckley, F. (1981) *Social audit: A management tool for co-operative working*, Leeds: Beechwood College.

Standing, G. (2014) *The precariat: The new dangerous class*, London: Bloomsbury.

Steinman, S. (2010) *An exploratory study into factors influencing an enabling environment for social enterprises in South Africa*, Geneva: International Labour Organization.

Stier, H., Lewin-Epstein, N. and Braun, M. (2001) 'Welfare regimes, family-supportive policies and women's employment along the life course', *American Journal of Sociology*, 106(6): 1731–60.

Stoker, G. (2005) 'New localism and the future of local governance: implications for the voluntary sector', in C. Robb (ed) *Voluntary action: meeting the challenges of the 21st century*, London: NCVO, pp 47–68.

Stokes, K., Clarence, E., Anderson, L. and Rinne, A. (2014) *Making sense of the UK collaborative economy*, London: NESTA.

Strauss, S. (2011) 'Ravitch: the problem with Teach For America', *Washington Post*, 15 February. Available from: http://voices.washingtonpost.com/answer-sheet/diane-ravitch/ravitch-the-problem-with-teach.html [accessed 22 September 2017].

Summers, L. H. (2016) 'The age of secular stagnation: what it is and what to do about it', *Foreign Affairs*, 15 February. Available from: www.foreignaffairs.com/articles/united-states/2016-02-15/age-secular-stagnation [accessed 30 October 2016].

Svallfors, S. (ed) (2012) *Contested welfare states: Welfare attitudes in Europe and beyond*, Stanford, CA: Stanford University Press.

Taylor-Gooby, P. (ed) (2004) *New risks, new welfare: The transformation of the European welfare state*, Oxford: Oxford University Press.

Teach First (nd) 'Our history', Available from: https://www.teachforamerica.org/about-us/our-story/our-history [accessed 28 August 2017].

Teasdale, P. (2011) 'What's in a name? Making sense of social enterprise discourses', *Public Policy and Administration*, 27(2): 1–22.

Therborn, G. (1986) *Why some people are more unemployed than others: The strange paradox of growth and unemployment*, London: Verso.

Thomson, J. (2017) 'Taking tips from the 2016 Homeless World Cup'. Available from:www.scott-moncrieff.com/news/news-updates/taking-tips-from-the-2016-homeless-world-cup [accessed 28 August 2017].

Thornhill, J. (2009) *Transforming estates*, Coventry: Chartered Institute of Housing.

Tidd, J., Bessant, J. and Pavitt, K. (2001) *Managing innovation* (2nd edn), Chichester: Wiley.

Toffler, A. (1984) *The third wave*, London: Bantam.

Torry, M. (2013) *Money for everyone: Why we need a citizen's income*, Bristol: Policy Press.

Tunstall, T. (2013) *Changing lives: Gustavo Dudamel, El Sistema, and the transformative power of music*, London: W. W. Norton & Company.

Utting, P. (2013) 'Social and solidarity economy: Pathway to socially sustainable development?' Available from: www.unrisd.org/unrisd/website/newsview.nsf/(httpNews)/AB920B156339500AC1257B5C002C1E96?OpenDocument [accessed 19 May 2015].

Veit-Wilson, J. (2102) 'Heading back to the poor law?' Available from: www.poverty.ac.uk/articles-attitudes-benefits-welfare-system-editors-pick/heading-back-poor-law [accessed 2 November 2016].

Von Hippel, E. (1988) *The sources of innovation*, Oxford: Oxford University Press.

Voorberg, W. H., Bekkers, V. J. and Tummers, L. G. (2014) 'A systematic review of co-creation and co-production: embarking on the social innovation journey', *Public Management Review*, 17(9): 1333–57.

Weil, D. (2014) *The fissured workplace: Why work became so bad for so many and what can be done to improve it*, Cambridge, MA: Harvard University Press.

Westley, F. and Antadze, N. (2010) 'Making a difference: strategies for scaling social innovation for greater impact', *Innovation Journal*, 15(2): article 2. Available from: www.innovation.cc/scholarly-style/ westley2antadze2make_difference_final.pdf [accessed 2 November 2016].

William-Powlett, K. (2014) *What to think about when you want to innovate: A brief guide for voluntary sector organisations.* London: Children's Partnership/NCVO.

Williams, R. C. (2007) *The cooperative movement: Globalization from below*, London: Routledge.

Wright, S. and Haux, T. (2001) *On the receiving end: Perspectives on being out of work and claiming benefits*, London: Child Poverty Action Group.

Young Foundation (2012) *Social innovation overview: A deliverable of the project: 'The theoretical, empirical and policy foundations for building social innovation in Europe' (TEPSIE), European Commission, 7th Framework Programme*, Brussels: European Commission, DG Research.

Yunus, M. (2008) *Creating a world without poverty: How social business can transform our lives*, New York: PublicAffairs.

Index

Z